SEA-FENCE!™

The Story of Big Lo, Super Fan

Lorin "Big Lo" Sandretzky

Merrell Publishing Company, LLC

Seattle, WA

Published by Merrell Publishing Company, LLC
701 Fifth Avenue, Suite 3520
Seattle WA   98104

info@merrellpublishing.com

First Edition.

ISBN 978-1503257221

Printed in the United States of America.

Disclaimer

This book is presented solely for entertainment purposes and is not to be considered as a resource for any other reason. The author and Merrell Publishing Company, LLC, have made every effort to ensure that the information in this book was correct at press time, and the author and publisher do not assume and hereby disclaim any liability to any party for any loss, damage, or disruption caused by errors or omissions, whether such errors or omissions result from negligence, accident, or any other cause.

The author has tried to recreate events, locales and conversations from his memories of them. In order to maintain their anonymity, in some instances the names of individuals and places may have been changed, or some identifying characteristics and details such as physical properties, occupations and places of residence may have been altered.

Best efforts have underscored the writing of this book, but the author and publisher make no representations or warranties of any kind and assume no liabilities of any kind with respect to the accuracy or completeness of the contents, and specifically disclaim any implied warranties of use for any particular purpose.

Neither the author nor Merrell Publishing Company, LLC, shall be held liable or responsible to any person or entity with respect to any loss or incidental or consequential damages caused, or alleged to have been caused, directly or indirectly, by the information contained in this book, or disruption caused by errors or omissions, whether such errors or omissions result from negligence, accident, or any other cause.

Dedication

To the memory of my mother, Marilou, who died of cancer when I was seven years young...

God, for creating everything I love in life...

Dad, for being the best Father a guy could ask for.

Bonnie and Scott, for everything every time I end up in the hospital.

Marlee and the kids, (Brittnee, Michael and Steffen) for the incredible times we've had together and all of your help with wound changes.

Christina and Boys (Jared and Christian) for being an amazing part of my life...

Merrell Publishing Company

Do you know someone who wants their book published?

Merrell Publishing Company is a Seattle publisher dedicated to providing full service book development. Whether you've already written your book and want it edited and prepared for publication, or you've been nurturing an idea for a book but just don't have the time to write, edit, publish, and market your own material...Merrell Publishing can do all or any of this for you.

Our staff of exceptional writers and editors will partner with you to create a book that provides the satisfaction and pride of being an author, in any subject you choose.

If you are:
- A professional who wants to become a published author
- A person with a great story to tell about your life
- A business owner enthusiastic about generating new clients and increased income
- A person wanting to teach others about your special skill or interest

... Merrell can produce your book — from concept to finished product, or anywhere in between— at an exceptionally reasonable cost.

As a boutique publisher, we'll help you tell your story with our customized approach. Whether your book is 100 or 500 pages, we can serve you from A to Z, and bring your book to life.

Please visit us at www.merrellpublishing.com and let's have a conversation!

Other Great Books by the Merrell Publishing Company

Available Now:

- Exit Insight: Getting to "Sold!"
- 401(k) Insight: Getting to "Retired!"
- Understanding Reverse Mortgages

New Books Coming Soon!

- Investment Insight: Getting to "Diversified!"
- Start-up Insight: Getting to "Funded!"

Acknowledgments

I wish to personally thank the following people:

For this Book:

Chris Egan and King 5, for your welcome and kind support throughout the years; **Joe Maas**, publisher and friend; thank you for helping me fulfill my dream by publishing my first book; **Dr. Daniel Levine**, my editor; your expertise, enthusiasm, dedication and patience were invaluable to the success of this book; **Tony DeLisio** for the great front cover design and being my friend and a great musician; **Chris Scott** for your excellent technical layout and back cover design; **Anika Klix**, associate editor, for your many hours of fine work and careful attention to detail; **Zander Levine**, assistant editor, for your insightful comments and editing suggestions.

Family:

Bonnie and Marlee, my dear sisters, and **Dad**, for all the months of nursing me and changing the bandages several times a day; without you, I know I would not have survived; and **Scott Mayer**, my best friend since we were babies.

My Friends in the Media:

Rod Simons for dubbing me Seattle's Biggest Sports Fan; **Bill Wixey** for a lot of Blue Friday fun; **Aaron Levine** of Q13; **Les Carpenter,** former Seattle Times sports writer; **Carolyn Douglas** for The Take a Bite out of the Big Apple Interview in 2001; **Xan Dewar** for all your help with the Big Sports Lo-Down and **Alan McElroy** for the opportunity.

My Friends in Sports:

Sonics guy **Kris Brannon** for keeping the Sonics fight alive; **Brian Robinson** and **Stephan Pyeatt** for trying to Save Our Sonics; **Nate McMillan** for everything; **George Karl** for being an amazing coach; the Sonicsgate guys: **Adam Brown,**

Jason Reid, Colin Baxter, Colin White, Darren Lund, Ian Connors; and all the kids (**my athletes!**)I've ever coached for helping me stay sober!

My Doctors:

Dr. Merrill, Dr. Greenan, and **Dr. Bagatell.**

And Just a Few of My Other Great Friends:

There are so many more friends I could put here, so if you're not listed, PLEASE know you are in my heart and I truly appreciate you!

Christian Burgess and **Jacknut Apparel**; **Rick Burgess** and **Coastline Signs; Scott Davis;** the **Cool Kids** at Diecutstickers.com; **Jim and Jeff** at Foamheads.com; Derm F/X's **Rod Hart** and **Cody Hart; Chentelle Hitchcock; Jerry Thornton** at Seattle Tackle Twill for finding jerseys in MY SIZE!; **Ahmed Imran** for video you've done for me; **Sacred Soul Scotty Tague** , **Michelle Haley; Roy Engelbrect** for giving me the ring announcing job; **Sam Perkins** for my nickname; **Louie Galarza** of Louie G's; **Jeff Dean** and Federal Way Panera Bread; **Dale Newman** at The Massage Clinic; **Bobby Barber** for that clean head haircut; **Jane** at Orchid Nails; and **Vic, Colby** and **Steve Payment** and the boys at Budget Auto Wrecking: you found me an engine... now can you find me a mechanic?!

And **Aunt Bonnie** for making me realize I'm somebody.

Foreword

The first time I met Seattle's Biggest Sports Fan was in September 2000, just two weeks after I arrived in Seattle as a sports reporter/anchor at Northwest Cable News. I was broadcasting live from Key Arena before a big SuperSonics game, and I was introduced to Big Lo. This giant of a man joined me during the live newscast, and the broadcast became pure magic. He was big, he was knowledgeable, he was loud and he was passionate about his team. After the live shot was over, I recall a producer asking me, "Who was that? He was awesome!" I said, "His name is Big Lo, Seattle's Biggest Sports Fan!" Since that day, Big Lo and I have had the pleasure of crossing paths and sharing amazing moments at hundreds of sporting events around the Northwest, events of all kinds and at all levels of play. Big Lo's love for the Seahawks, Storm, Sounders, Mariners and Mist is unparalleled.

Over the past decade there seems to be one constant with Seattle sports teams, and it's that Big Lo is there supporting the team, win or lose. He truly is Seattle's Biggest Sports Fan...but there is something much bigger than his 6'8" stature or his booming voice that can be heard from Puyallup to Poulsbo. Big Lo has distinguished himself through the immensity of his "heart". He asks for nothing and yet he always gives so much.

While most people only see Big Lo as "that big sports fan" that's always at all the games, I've had the great pleasure of seeing a whole other side of Big Lo. I've seen the Big Lo who came down to cheer Bonney Lake High School students during an assembly, I've seen the Big Lo that showed up late to a Turkey Bowl football game because he was busy delivering food to those in need, I've seen the Big Lo who auctioned off his Seahawks tickets to serve great causes, I've seen the Big Lo at the airport at 2:00 a.m. cleaning the ice and snow off SuperSonics players' cars, I've seen the Big Lo coaching young kids in football, and I've also seen the Big Lo sick and fighting for his life in a hospital bed, more worried about how his Seattle sports teams were doing than his own health.

Over the years, players and coaches will come and go, but Big Lo is always here. Whether it's the third row, first-base side, 300-level, or front row with a SEA-FENCE™ sign, Big Lo is here, rain or shine, and more times than not in the rain! Sure, some would call Big Lo a lucky man because of his unending love for everything about sports, but in the end I believe we are the ones that hit the jackpot with Big Lo! He gives, cheers, gives more, cheers harder, gives even more and cheers even harder…and then starts all over again. His passion and pride are infectious, but what's most important to me…what matters more to me than any victory on the court, field or pitch, is my friendship with this wonderful, unique, and compassionate man.

"Just another sports fan," you say?

Hardly.

He's Big Lo, Seattle's Biggest Sports Fan!

Chris Egan, King 5 TV Sports Anchor/Reporter

Four-Time Emmy® Award Winner

Winner of the Edward R. Murrow Award for Sports Reporting

Contents

Introduction

Hi! I'm Big Lo. You may have seen me around CenturyLink Field, or maybe at some other sports event. My nickname is Big Lo because I'm kind of a big guy! Actually, Sam Perkins, the former Seattle SuperSonic, dubbed me Big Lo. I'm 6'8", and these days I weigh 365 pounds, but I wasn't always this thin. I'll tell you all about that later in this book, but for now what I really want to say is that I'm glad you're reading this because I think there's a lot of good stuff in here, not just about me, but also about our Seattle teams.

I'll bet you and I are similar in a lot of ways, because we both like sports, and we love our teams and the athletes on those teams, and somehow sports mean a lot to you, just like they do to me. You and I, we have the power, Fan Power, and what that means to me is that we can do good for our teams, and just as importantly, we can do good for our communities and ourselves. When you read this book, you'll see what I mean.

Just to let you know, this book is not only about me. It's also about you and me, and what we can do to help each other, help those around us, and to make the lives of the people we meet better in every way we can. You and I, we have passion, and lots of energy! With that power and strength come the opportunity and even the obligation to bring goodness, health, support, and love to the people we know and the people we don't know who need our love and support. I used to be a hellion, but everything changed for me as I got older and smarter. This is my story, but it's really about all of us because I believe each one of us has a story of challenge, change, and the chance to grow better and brighter.

Thank you for reading my story. If you see me in the stands, or at a fundraising event, or on the street, please come up and say hi. I'd love to meet you and shake your hand.

Best wishes today and always, Big Lo.
November, 2014

Big Lo Sundays

There's nothing like being with 68,000 of your closest friends. Sunday game days are probably the best days of the week for me. Sundays used to be a church-day for me, but now it seems like my church has become CenturyLink Field and being with all those people, cheering on our favorite team, the Seattle Seahawks. Our fans are the best in the whole world!

There's nothing like being in our stadium because of the passion and the camaraderie and the fever you get in anticipation of the game, and then once kickoff comes, the energy and excitement magnifies with thousands of people, and everybody gets so pumped up! It's fun to be part of the crowd and being loud on game days, and having fun with all your friends.

Morning comes early on game days. Sometimes I wake up about 4:00 a.m. because I can't sleep, I'm so hungry for game time. Sometimes I sleep in until 4:15 or 4:30, but I usually get up at 4:00, take a good hot shower and get ready to go. I always make sure I've got the Sea-Fence™ sign, my Lynch jersey, and my game day bag. In the bag, I throw in my gloves; these are the receiver gloves I wear to protect my hands because when I'm smacking the signs I can get big old blisters. If it's going to be a hot day, I bring this little portable fan with a sprayer on it to keep me cool; it's awesome. If it's going to be a cold day, I'll bring my sideline jacket, like the players wear. I make sure I have ibuprofen for when I get a little sore during the second or third quarter; my shoulders get a bit stiff, as I'm still waiting for a double shoulder replacement, and a lot of people like to slap me on my shoulders during the game! I take along a bottle of 5-hour Energy in case my energy gets depleted, and I always take along a couple of extra pens in case I see a kid trying to get an autograph who doesn't have a pen, or if I want something signed, too. There are just so many different things that are helpful to have for game day, so I bring along my little bag of tricks.

Then I go outside into the cool morning air, get in the Jeep, and head down to the stadium, usually arriving around 5:30 or 6:00 a.m., and I park next to my buddy Al's Gourmet Hot Dogs food truck. Al's been letting me park next to him for, gosh, 15 years or so. It's nice to be able to park right across from the stadium, knowing your vehicle is safe when you go inside. I meander around for a little bit, go tailgating, talk to the fans, get high fives and hugs, and take pictures of people and with people, and it's just quite an honor to be as well-known a fan as I am because it seems like 99.9% of the people love me. There's that 0.1% that seem to despise who I am, but they don't really know me. That's one of the reasons I want to tell my story, so people know I'm really not such a bad guy!

You might think it's kind of early to be down there by 6:00 a.m. for an afternoon game, but that's my mission. There are people even crazier than me because some folks tailgate down there all night long! The stadium gates open at 10:00 a.m., about three hours before game time. As soon as security opens the gates, that's when we go in!

These days, the first crowd in the door is about 2,000 people. A couple of years ago only about five or 10 people came in that early (I'm being facetious), but now you have a big group of people waiting for the gates to open, and it's great! This is what our athletes should have been experiencing for the last 38 years...

I don't eat or drink before games because when you put something in, it's gotta go out, and I don't want to miss anything! One of my game day rituals is I've got a bag of almonds I eat for energy during the games. Shannon Love sits to my right (also known as the Super Fan, Mr. Love) and he's always got food; he normally brings a couple of containers of protein shakes, and usually gives me one of them; that gives me extra energy to get through the game. Occasionally my buddy Spike's brother, Kevin, brings me little Snacker sandwiches, and

I take my chances by taking a bite or three, but it's fine with me as far as not eating until after the game.

I go in when they open the gates. Lately there have been a lot of people going in early because people want to get autographs and experience all the different parts of being at a game because there's more to it than just the game itself. It's the excitement that surrounds it, it's the pregame hype, it's watching the players warm up and occasionally they'll come over and say hi to you, and see what you're up to.

"How's life?"

 "All right!"

"Well, good! Have a good day."

And you wish them a good game and "See you later", you know? Some days they have a good game, and some days they have a great game!

Before I go to my seat, I go over and say hi to the ladies at the information booth. Jamie, Shannon and Julia are awesome! Every game they greet me with a smile. I say my hellos and get my free drink coupon; there's a designated driver program and since I don't drink alcohol, it's nice not to have to pay $4.00 for a bottle of water at the games. When you sign-up as a designated driver, you get a free water or soda and that's kind of like one of my rituals. I get my free soda, go down to my seat, and I wait for the first player that comes over and says hi.

This is my 26th year having season tickets. I started going early, when I was young. My aunt's the one who got me into being a Seahawks' fan. Before the Seahawks, I was a Minnesota Vikings fan because Dad was from Duluth, Minnesota; he was a big Purple People Eater fan back in the late '60s and early 70s, so we always watched the Vikings on game days. My Aunt Rinkie absolutely loves her Vikings!

Then in 1976, all of a sudden, BOOM! we have a team! I love the Seahawks and I've been passionate about them since the beginning. I've gone to the games for years and years, but I started getting season tickets in 1988. My seat number is Section 122, Row A, Seats 1 and 2. I've got two seats so I can bring a friend. Even though I have two seats, I'm hardly ever sitting down!

When the stadium management took us on the first tours of the new stadium, they told me they had a lot of requests from fans who wanted to sit by or near me, and I felt quite honored by that. I was in the first fan group that went into the stadium. I was with Mama Blue, and some of the guys in the front row that sit next to me now, like Paco, AKA Bam Bam, or Hair Dude, and my front row brothers, Darryl, Brandon, and Matt. It was just a really neat experience that we got to do something like that. So I took a sign with me that said, "First Sign in Seahawk Stadium" and that's now kind of a classic.

Surrounding me and nearby are other Super Fans. Like I said, to my right is Shannon Love who's known as Mr. Love with his white hat, flashy suit, and shades. Next to him is the Seahulk in his hard hat and his amazing muscles. Then, to my left, is Jeff and Dede Schumaier, who are Mr. and Mrs. Seahawk with their blue and green hair and Seahawk logo on their faces... they sit down the way, and then there's Kiltman, that's Neil Hart; Painted Hawk is Bruce McMillan... Brad and Laura Carter are Cannonball and Hawkychick; and Mama Blue, she's Patti Hammond; Mr. Mohawk is Phil Andrus. There was also HawkFiend; Bryan Murphy was a big part of my life in 2008; he and a bunch of people got together and did a benefit for me to raise some money when I was very sick. I think he's got a job in middle-America somewhere now and I haven't heard from him in a long time, but I bet he's still a Seahawks fan.

I'm surrounded by a lot of Super Fans! Heck, as far as I'm

concerned, all 68,000 of us are Super Fans! Behind me are Rob and RJ, Rob's wife, my big buddy Nate, Robin, Jeff, Stu and the gang...and I consider all these people family. I'm also just learning this year about a couple of new Super Fans I've never seen before, and friends say, "Oh yeah, they've been sitting there for years," and I wish I would've met them before. There are 68,000 people here, and it's hard to meet everybody!

So after I get to my seat, it's not long before the guys are stretching out and warming up. I'm about four feet off the field, and the players are about 15 or 20 feet away. I'm in the south end zone. That's where our team goes to start stretching; it's always been that way...since the beginning of time! I always give them some encouragement like, "Have a great game," or "This is your day!" There are all kinds of things I say to build them up and besides, it's game day so you want to fire them up and get them ready.

Usually the practice squad comes out first. They stretch out with their strength and conditioning coaches. Next comes the punter and the long snapper, and they're followed by a few of the defensive backs, the linebackers. Then all of a sudden out pops Marshawn Lynch and he's got this really cool little mask-thing he wears, and I think it's like a breathing apparatus so he can breathe in fresh air but I'm not quite sure exactly what it is. Hopefully one day I'll get to ask him what it is and see what it does. He comes out looking like Darth Vader! He's got his hoodie up and over his head and all you see is this mask-thing sticking out in front of him, and the crowd erupts! There are fans waiting for autographs, and there are also fans doing the same thing I'm doing, being cool and just taking it all in, taking in the ambiance. Marshawn kind of marches around the field; it's his energizer. Then out come Richard Sherman and Kam Chancellor. When they come out the crowd erupts again, and it's really cool to be part of this and see what the pregame is for the guys as well as the fans.

Most people don't know that the warm-ups begin about two or

two-and-a-half hours before game time. At first the athletes come out individually and do their own personal routine. Each guy has his own warm-up and exercise sets. Then they go back in for a little while, for about 10 or 15 minutes, and put on their uniforms...their jerseys, shoulder pads, and all that stuff. Then they come out as units and you get to see all the special teams, all the defensive backs, and all the linemen. Now each of these units does team warm-ups. That's when they go through their stretching and warm-ups together. Then they'll do little group practice sessions, and then first team and second-team routines which is when they run through plays and other practice sets. Our guys are on the south end of the field, and the other team will be on the north side of the stadium, near the Hawks' Nest. I love having a seat in the end zone, because I get to watch our guys work out during pregame, and even though I don't see the plays develop like I would if I were in the upper seats and the seats around the sides, but if you know the game, you know how the play is going to develop. It's really fun to be in the end zone because when our team scores a touchdown right in front of you, it's amazing! I've had guys run and jump into my arms, I've had touchdown balls thrown to me...there's nothing like being as close to the game as we are!

About a half hour before game time, team warm-ups are still going on, and the teams are running through their plays. There are probably about 25-30,000 fans in the stands by now and you can feel that energy, that warmth, that fever, and the anticipation of game time is so much closer because it's only 30 - 40 minutes away.

Then the players all group up together, they do a team cheer with "Seahawks!" on the count of three, and then they run into the locker room for their last pregame details before team introductions begin.

In the meantime, there is usually a special event. There might be a presentation for player awards, like the Steve Largent Award or maybe special recognition for someone in our community who has done some excellent volunteer work or made some big contribution that's helped lots of people. I like that because I believe that recognition and gratitude for someone's efforts inspire other people to do good deeds; we all need a helping hand sometimes. So that's a really important part of the pregame experience.

The Sea Gals are also an important part of the pregame show. Each of them is very pretty and the eye candy for the team. For me, I'm all about the game, but I love the Sea Gals and what they do for the community. They're not like cheerleaders in high school, though that's part of it. They add to the fans' excitement, and they're always shaking their pom-poms and have big pretty smiles, and they perform an on-field show, kind of like a dance. They sometimes have a dance routine to modern songs, sometimes older songs, and it's always cool to see their smiles and how the kids and guys light up to them, so it's part of the fun, part of the ambience.

Why I really like them is because they do so many good things in the community. They make a swim suit calendar that raises money for women's shelters, and they do a charity auction toward the end of the year to raise money for community needs, so it's really neat that they actively use their influence to help others. We need to cheer them on, too!

After the Sea Gals' dance performance, the team introductions begin. The stadium announcer says, "Let's introduce the visiting team", and a lot of the fans boo. I don't like it, because I think it gives the visiting team extra fire, and adds to how badly they want to win. But I understand it, and it's fun for the fans that like to do that, so it's all good. The thing is though, I can't boo. It's something I've never been able to do.

Next, the stadium announcer builds up the excitement, and there's a big puff of smoke and running onto the field come our guys! Our Seahawk players are introduced and the crowd cheers, applauds, and goes wild!

Now it's time for the Star-Spangled Banner. The singing of the national anthem is really an amazing moment. It's how we honor our country, and each singer is different, and sings it a little bit differently. Sometimes it's a big-name person, and sometimes it's a person you don't know, but it's still such an honor to be able to be with that many people who love our country. It's really amazing. A lot of times I'll get a chill down my spine when I hear those words and the emotion behind them. It's an important moment in the experience of the game, and one more thing that builds up the excitement. I love it!

After the national anthem and before the kickoff is the coin toss. Sometimes during the coin toss the players are joined by a young kid who's going through some kind of health issue or has some kind of adversity. It's got to be a real special feeling for the kids to be out there, and it makes you warm inside to see a kid receive an honor like that.

Years ago there was a young boy named Max, and he had the flesh eating bacteria like I did, so he got to do some ceremonial activities with the Seahawks, the Mariners and the Sonics, I think. He was a really neat boy and I kept in contact with him for a long time. I remember he survived the disease, but we've lost contact.

It used to be that whoever won the coin toss wanted the ball first. It seems like these days we're in such a defensive-minded football world that everybody wants to defer, so when they do the coin toss, you're hoping your team wins the toss so they can defer and get the ball in the second half. If that happens, the defense comes onto the field after the kickoff.

It's game time! Once the kicker connects with the ball, the crowd goes crazy and you hear the big loud WHOOSH and it's kind of like a bomb going off! It's an explosion of excitement! It's really cool because the player gets the ball and makes his way up the field, but hopefully not too far if it's the other team! Holy smokes! It's an amazing feeling to feel the pulse of the crowd because you know everybody's going to get loud, and that's our mission...to be as loud as we can to energize our guys. There's nothing quite like the feeling of that much energy!

Some games are like a roller coaster ride. You feel as though the other team is performing as well as your team, and then all a sudden that team scores and you're frustrated because you didn't want them to. Then our team scores and everything's good again, and then all of a sudden our team intercepts the ball and you're feeling really good and the team scores and now we're in the lead and feeling even happier. But you never know how the game is going to end up. There's that saying by Bert Bell about "any given Sunday." That's so true because on any given Sunday your team can play great or your team can play poorly, and sometimes the game goes against us. You have to deal with the wins and with the losses.

After the game there's always a group of players from both teams that get together in the center of the field and they say a prayer after the game. It's nice to see guys giving God His due respect. Playing this game takes a lot of determination and sometimes we need the help that comes from above because it helps us perform better and be better people. It's nice to see the guys get in the center of the field to say a prayer, and then some of the guys meander off and say hi to their buddies on the other team.

The hugging and high-fiving in the stands is fun. I have friends that come down to visit with me after the game. Each game they want to say hi, so here comes my buddy, J.P., and he's always asking what's up. There are also the friendly goodbyes, and "See ya next game!", and there's so much to it that it just kind of ends up in a blur at the end. You say so many hi's and bye's and then

you think, "Oh shoot, did I say hi to so-and-so?" and you feel
bad because they were standing there and you saw them and
didn't get a chance to say hi to them! So it leaves me with a
feeling like, oh, boy, that feeling of emptiness when you left
somebody out. That's the hard part about leaving the stadium; I
don't want to leave anybody out of a high-five or a hug or a hand
shake!

After the game, I go down to the post-game area and visit with
the players and give that extra love to them. "Great game! You
did amazing today!" There are so many different ways to say
congratulations to a player after a good game and you want to
say the right words. Usually I get to say hi in the players' family
area. I always say hi to Mama Sherman, and I try to say hi to
Richard Sherman's brother, Branton. It's part of the game day
experience.

After the players come out of the locker room they're tired and
want to go home, so I don't want to bug them and keep them for
long periods of time; they want to go out to dinner with their
families or go home and just relax, so I head out. If the traffic's
still going, I wait for it to die down a little. If traffic's not going, I
get in my jeep and mosey down the road on the dusty trail...

When our team loses, I stay positive because as frustrating as it
is to lose the game, you have to stay strong and know that our
team is going to do a great job in the next game. I'm usually
trying to keep everybody's head up and lift them emotionally.
It's just one game and we can win the next one. If it's two
games, three games or ten games that are lost, you still have to
have that same admiration for the team because you want the
guys to see you happy. Some people get upset by a loss, and
wonder how I can accept it. I don't see why anybody would want
to dwell on the negative when you can be happy with the
positive. I'm always grateful we have such a wonderful team,
and I'm grateful I get to see them play! I try to analyze every
game with the pluses and the minuses, but it just seems to me

that the positives always outweigh the negatives.

Now that the game is over, I'm famished and pretty hungry so it's time to get something to eat. A lot of times I'll go to my friends in Burien, the Ramos family, who have a Mexican restaurant called La Costa. Hilda and her family serve great home-style dinners, so we go there and eat, and I get a little dinner to go for Dad. When I get home, Dad and I talk about the game for a little while, and then I start watching the Sunday night game with him until I fall asleep.

That's how my Sunday game days usually go.

My Life as Lorin

It seems like my interest in competition started with marbles.
Back in the day, as a kid, we played marbles. I used to be very
competitive with my best friend Scotty, and we played all the
time. We'd go to school with just a couple of marbles and come
home with our pockets bulging. All of us wanted to play this one
kid, Dale Fuskerud. He had more marbles than anyone had
anything. This was from kindergarten until third grade when I
dropped marbles and got into playing soccer. I played for the
Puget Sound Soccer Club, and later I had fun with baseball.

The very first sporting event I saw was a Sonics game, and this
opened my eyes. I was elated with seeing professional sports
competition and I began to understand what sports was really
about, and how as a player this is where you strive to be in your
future. I knew I wanted to play with these guys, so that was
when I got my love for team sports; it was playing soccer,
baseball, and then going to my first Sonics game. Later that year
I went to a Sounders match at Memorial Stadium in the Seattle
Center and, man, I loved everything about it. When I got to high
school, I joined the football team and loved that feeling of
comradery, of being part of a team, having a place and a
purpose, of being in this together, and so my love of sports
started when I was young.

I was about six or seven years old when Dad was doing the flat
work for the Kingdome, back when it was being built in the early
'70s and Mom was still alive. I used to hang out a lot with Dad;
I'd go to work with him, and I'd sit in a pile of dirt somewhere
and make little tracks with my Hot Wheels and create war
scenes with my army men. There were times when he'd yell and
say, "Hey, come here!" and I'd run over and leave my army men
and cars. The next thing I knew, some other guy in another
bulldozer had bulldozed over them and all of a sudden it's "
Noooooo!" So I had these dramatic moments when my toys got
buried under what later became the Kingdome, and here I am,

40 years later and realizing, holy smokes, that's sacred ground under there! Dad also did excavation work for the Columbia Towers and his job was to dig the hole, so he was way down in that thing; I think it was over 130 feet deep...but I didn't get to play in that hole!

I have two sisters, Marlee and Bonnie. Marlee is 4 years older, and Bonnie is 10 years older. My mom battled cancer for six years and we lost her in 1973. When she passed away it just seemed like I was lost because she was like my best friend. She always made sandwiches for all my friends in the neighborhood, and she took all of us to the hobby store so we could get marbles, and especially the ones we called oversizers, which were these extra big marbles. Mom was my buddy, and when she passed away, it was devastating. I was seven years old so I just didn't understand it. I asked my dad where my mom was, when Mom was coming back, and he said, "Well, she went away for a while. She's on a vacation", and I didn't really grasp the meaning of that. When I was about 10 or 11 years old I said, "Dad, when's Mom coming back?" and he said, "Well, she's dead." That was when I realized what death was all about. It's permanent. It's forever.

Mom had told Dad to find somebody to take care of us kids, so he dated relatively soon after Mom passed, and he met a lady named Donna. They ended up marrying and she had four kids and we became the Brady Bunch. Donna was a really neat lady. The downside was that her boys were older and taught me to do some things I shouldn't have learned and didn't know how to do well, so I'd take money out of my sister's purse and get in trouble for it. Things like that. I don't remember how long Dad and Donna were married, but they ended up getting divorced.

Then Dad met a lady named Irene, and she had four kids, and they got married. But then a terrible thing happened. The week I found out I made the Little League All-Star team was when Irene said she wanted to move! Dad and Irene went house hunting, found a house in Kent, and we all moved. I was in Kent for almost four years, until the middle of ninth grade. It was awful because I had to leave my best friend, Scotty, behind in Burien, and my entire family, all my aunts, uncles, and cousins... Everyone I knew and loved was in Burien, and Kent seems like a million miles away when you're a kid, you know?

It was a hard adjustment at first because I didn't know anybody out there. I had no friends, so I didn't want to play sports. Any kid who ever had to leave their home understands how awful this was, because I had to make all new friends, find new places to hang out, new things to do... It was a traumatic time in my life because I'd just found out I had made the All-Star team for the first time and I was absolutely ecstatic about that...but I never got to play. I heard they had a really good All-Star season and ended up playing for the regional championship! I missed the whole thing, and this hurt extra bad.

Eventually I integrated into the Kent community. I went to Meridian Elementary and made some incredible friends. Then after sixth grade, I went to Sequoia Junior High and played football for the Sequoia Junior High Cherokees. I was an offensive lineman. Then our coach, Howie Martin, had a heart attack during one of the games and died on the sidelines. They took him away in an ambulance but couldn't revive him, so that was a very emotional time in my life. Coach Martin was somebody I looked up to and was close with, and that's when I realized that my sports passion was more intense than other peoples, because it seemed like it hit me harder than any of the other kids on the team. Maybe it was also because my mom died when I was very young and my dad had remarried twice, and I felt uprooted from my family and friends. But I dwelled on my newest loss for a good five or six months before I could get past it; I really took it hard.

After the first half of ninth grade we moved back to Burien, so we were back in the family home again. My dad had rented it out while we were in Kent. Boy, it was good to be back! I went to Puget Sound Junior High for the last half of the year.

I reconnected with a lot of my old buddies and I made some new ones as well. It was scary at first because there I was, leaving all the friends I had in Kent, and then I was back in Burien, but I was excited because at least Scotty was going to be there, you know? I was looking forward to being with my best friend again. He's been with me my whole life so there was Scotty's smiling face, yelling, "Yeah! You're back in the 'hood!" That made the transition a whole lot easier.

Things had changed, people come and people go and that's one of the hard things, losing the friends you knew for your first six years of school, and then all a sudden they've moved elsewhere. I lost a lot of friends but having Scotty there made it so much easier. He introduced me to all the new people in the neighborhood and that's how I met Gary Hall and Eddie Poyneer. My good buddy Paul Wisniewski was still a couple of houses up the hill. It was really neat to be back around my buddies, the people that really loved me.

It wasn't long before I was in Evergreen High School. The high school years were fun but challenging because I didn't know what I wanted to do. Mostly, I just wanted to play football. I was playing bass guitar out in the hallway by the choir class one day when the choir teacher came by. We were talking for a few minutes and he said, "Well, why don't you sing?" And I said, "Sing? I can't sing." He said, "Can you talk?" and I said, "Yes", and he said, "Well, then, you can sing!"

I'd always sung by myself at the house so I knew I could carry a tune, but I thought, "Uh, choir? Isn't that for sissies?" Well, I became a sissy! I was probably one of the best singers in the choir. My voice range was low to very, very high. I could sing as high as the highest sopranos in the choir. That always made people laugh. So then I was in the concert choir. I was in

Chanteurs, which is a show choir, and before long I ended up in a barbershop quartet. I just really loved to sing, and still do.

High school was rugged because I didn't study as hard as I should have. It's one of the biggest messages I try to get across to kids is that you have to do your studies and succeed in school, because that's the most important time in your life. It's your education and at that point in life, for the most part, your education is free. Well, it was then! I look back and think, "Why didn't I study more?" Some people say you don't need to study certain subjects because you won't need the information in the future, but I think you really do because there are things I look back on and think, "Wow, I wish I would've studied that more because I could use it now!"

I would have loved to study math more. Once I hit algebra it got boring, and then it was on to calculus. I didn't like to do the work because it taxed my mind, and I wanted to be doing other things like hanging out with my buddies, or playing video games. I also liked playing football, so math and my other school work took a back seat.

I joined the football team and became the left offensive tackle. In those days I loved to hit people. This was how I could get all my aggressions out and not get in trouble...but I kept my aggressions on the field. I was afraid to get into fights because I didn't want to hurt people, and besides, I was always the bigger guy.

Playing football was great! I loved having fun out there on the field. It was also great being part of something bigger than myself, bonding with my team, having athletic male friends, and seeing the fans in the stands cheer for us whether we won or lost. It taught me a lot. In my senior year in high school, we started the Wolverine Rowdy Rooters, and I was in this group. We yelled and screamed as loud as we could and got everybody on the team pumped up. The basketball games were a lot more fun because we would sit in the stands close to the court and scream and holler and make fools of ourselves, energizing the crowd. This is where I really learned the value and power of fan support for teams. It was the beginning of my fan-dom. I realized it was not about winning or losing...it was about supporting my team no matter what. High school gave me the experience of being an athlete on the football team, and being an active fan during the other sport seasons.

I played football in my sophomore, junior, and senior years. I was also in regional choir competitions; I had great ratings and was Best in the Northwest in '83-'84, and was in the Who's Who in music in 1984.

Pretty soon, it was time for high school graduation...but I couldn't graduate! The school's attendance rules stated a student could only miss 16 days to graduate, and I had missed 17. I missed one day too many and didn't get to graduate with my class. That was pretty devastating for me. About three years later I took the GED and that's how I finished. It was a pretty rough time because I really wanted to walk across that stage, but it wasn't meant to be.

Actually, because I suffered with that, I'm now a strong advocate for teaching kids the value of education and helping them build the determination to study hard, improve their mind, maintain good attendance, and learn as much as possible about everything. We live in a fascinating world and we're extremely fortunate to live in the United States where there is so much opportunity to sample everything. With a good education, you can choose what you need and create a peaceful and productive life.

Along with this comes our responsibility to pitch in and help others; we are a great nation of remarkable people. Each of us can do more, and be more, and it starts with education and being kind to each other.

The D-Fence Sign is Born

It was during my senior year, probably midway through the
Seahawks season. Scotty and I were walking home from school,
past the Pay 'N Save drug store in Burien. The big "D" from the
word "DRUG" had fallen off the building. It was about 4' x 4',
a real big D in a square block, because that's how Pay 'N Save
did their letters in those days. The D was white against a blue
background, lying up against this rickety picket fence that went
around an old folk's home behind the drugstore. As Scotty and I
were walking down this little lane, we spotted the big D against
that fence.

It suddenly hit me that the D and the ancient fence together
made the word "DEFENSE", so I said that out loud and Scotty
and I thought it was funny. That's when it occurred to me
to make a "D-Fence" sign to bring to the Seahawk game on
Sunday. My aunt had bought tickets for me to go to the game
that weekend against the Oakland Raiders, so I got a big sheet of
cardboard from some boxes in the back of the grocery store and
made this ugly D, and then I used another piece of cardboard
and I made a fence out of that. I made the fence so it looked like
a picket fence and it had five pointy slats. I painted the two signs
white with some poster paint I found lying around the house,
and Scotty and I went to the game with them. We thought it was
funny, but we never realized what an effect they would have.

During the pregame time, a cameraman saw us and came up to
Scotty and me. He asked, "Hey, what's the fence all about?" I
held it up and said, "D-Fence!" The cameraman said, "Holy
smokes, that's a great idea, kid! Did you copyright that?" "Uh,
no," I replied. "I'm an 18-year old kid!" The cameraman said
he'd never seen one at the stadium before; this was now my
thing to take to the games from then on. Sometimes I held the D
and Scotty held the fence, and sometimes we switched.

At this first game, some people didn't like us putting the signs up and blocking their view, so we kept them down for most of the game, but we'd put them up on defense and try to spark the crowd a bit. There were mixed reactions for a while, but it wasn't long before we became the D and Fence Dudes!

Scotty and I took the original D-Fence sign to home games only a few times, and stopped. We brought the sign back and, in the early '90s, I was introduced to foam core to make the sign, and that's when we used it hard-core and didn't miss a game with it. After they imploded the Kingdome, the Seahawks played in Husky Stadium and we had some real soaker games there. We used to get really wet at the games there, and the downpours were so bad that sometimes we went through two or three signs in the same game! The foam core just turned into this ugly paste. Soon after that we began using this stuff called corrugated plastic.

When I discovered the plastic it was like Lewis and Clark reaching the Pacific Ocean, like Alexander Graham Bell inventing the telephone, the neatest thing since sliced pickles, and I was excited as heck because the plastic was so much easier to cut. I could use a precision blade and trim-out the D and cut slats in the fence and, gosh, it was so much easier than making the signs out of cardboard!

We thought about doing something else fun...a few years ago we made an O-Fence sign, but there was another guy who made a big off-switch to go with his fence...Off-Fence. It was pretty funny!

I thought it was pretty cool when I started seeing the D-Fence sign on broadcasts from other stadiums! Besides, who's to say that somebody didn't have one at a basketball game or somewhere before me? I believe I was the first, but many people often think they were the one who started something; it's part of life that sometimes people get the same great ideas at the same time.

The original D-Fence sign got trashed after I moved out of my dad's house. When I moved out, my step-mom threw away all my old sports cards, and some special shoes that players had given me, and a whole bunch of stuff was put in the trash. Every kid has a story like that...it was crazy, just crazy, losing all those treasures!

Barbecue King

Once I was out of school, I had to find work. I'd had paper routes before, but my first real job was with Domino's Pizza, and that's where I learned how to make deliveries; I worked at Domino's for about four months. A buddy of mine was working at 3 Pigs BBQ in Burien and he said, "Hey, come in and apply!" So I applied for a job and started working there as a delivery driver, and I became the delivery driver extraordinaire because I knew the area so well. This was also where I began to learn how to cook barbecue.

After our shifts every night we'd head out to the parking lot until 1:00 – 2:00 in the morning, just playing touch football, having fun, being kids, being young. That was when the drinking side of life started up and we were all smoking pot, thinking we were cool and getting in trouble with the cops for loitering, being where we shouldn't be, drinking when we shouldn't be, and so we often had little run-ins with the cops from time to time.

I was making some cash, which was nice, and living at home, and that's the story for a year or two. Eventually, I moved out and moved in with Gary Hall, a buddy of mine. We shared an apartment for probably nine months or so. Life was easy, life was good; I bounced from place to place, living with my buddies, working...I went through my restaurant phase, and then my construction phase. I wanted to be like Dad, become a large machine operator or something, so I started out digging a lot of ditches and doing underground work, down in the trenches laying pipe.

That didn't develop into anything meaningful, so when I was 21 I moved to Poulsbo and started cooking barbecue. I became really serious about barbecue and I entered barbecue competitions with my buddy Bruce. We were winning championships, too, cooking barbecue and learning what competition was really about. The whole time I was traveling back and forth to Seahawk games. I made sure I got tickets for every game because it was so much fun, and I also went to all the Mariners games. As many games as I could go to, I went! Well, as many as I could afford, anyway. I lived out in Poulsbo so it was a ferry commute, but I loved my 'Hawks games.

The barbecue competitions were pretty intense. There is an organization called the Chili Appreciation Society International (CASI). They have competitions all across the United States. They raise money for charity and scholarships, and they have one heck of a good time while they do it! Bruce and I started cooking in chili competitions and chili cook-offs in our area, and then we heard they did barbecue competitions as well, so we started cooking competition barbecue. We did this for a couple of years.

As you can imagine, there's a lot that goes into a barbecue competition. You start with a hunk of meat and decide if you're going to do a dry rub, or no rub, or if you are you going to season it...all these decisions come into play. We always did a dry rub, so we'd get the meat all covered with our rub and then build a fire in our fire pit. Some folks want to smoke at a low temperature and cook it for a long time; we'd usually do 14 -18 hour smokes on big meats like briskets and pork butts. We'd do about a 4-6 hour smoke on our lighter meats like chicken and pork ribs, and then we'd just sit there and tend our fire all night. Every team has a spray bottle in case the fire comes up; you don't want to char your meat. There's a lot to it. All the barbecuing is done at the competition site.

There are usually about 20-25 teams in most competitions, with each team having anywhere from two to five people. Of course, the teams hang out all night, in the dark, watching their meats slowly cook, partying, drinking, smoking...you get the idea. They were a lot of fun!

Over the three or four years we did this, Bruce and I won several awards. We went to Tyler, Texas, and beat some big cooks there. We won Grand Champion several times; we did that back to back, and were also National Champions two years in a row. It wasn't that big a deal because it wasn't a world championship, but we did all right. Later we opened a restaurant in Poulsbo called Larry's Best BBQ and the local paper did a big news story on us.

We won a lot of trophies, ribbons and awards, and Bruce kept them all for us; we've lost touch with each other, and I don't know where he is! But we were a good team, and those are some great memories.

After that, I moved to Alki and lived there for almost a year. That's when I got involved with fighting City Hall, trying to keep cruising alive on Alki. That was my first exposure to the media. On any given Saturday or nice hot sunny Sunday, there were thousands of cars down there, cruising the strip, enjoying the rays, checking out the scene...and being seen! But the Seattle City Council wouldn't give us a chance. We wanted to show the adults in power that we were a group of young people that had it together, and we'd clean up the beach and make sure people were staying in check when they were doing their cruising thing. Cruising has been around for years, you know, they did it in the 50's and 60's and 70's...

So, there I was, battling Jane Noland and all the other City Council members, and my sister and this guy named Rob Halliday put together this group of people, and we blew up in the media because everybody wanted to interview us and talk to us about the situation. For a few years I was known as the "Alki Guy". The Council shot us down really quickly, though; that battle lasted probably six months and the Council created the anti-cruising ordinance anyway. Now people can't enjoy cruising the strip anymore, but it taught me the will to fight. It lit up my desire to battle and win. We didn't win, but it taught me a lot about politics, about the media, about how to organize and protest for change, and a whole lot about myself.

A Bouncer for the Clubs

This is a pretty interesting part of my life. My sister, Marlee, lived in this building that was kind of like a barn, and it was in the backyard of this guy's house in Tukwila. She decided she was going to go on the road, so I took over her apartment; it was like a loft. One night a buddy of mine was having a bachelor party, and it was going to be at this bar in downtown Seattle. I walked into the club, but I didn't know it was the wrong club. When I stepped in, my buddy, Tony, happened to be the DJ. He said, "Holy smokes, what are you doing here, man?"

 I got a big ol' handshake and a hug from him and I said, "I'm looking for my buddy. They're supposed to have a bachelor party here," and Tony said, "No, man, there are two clubs with the same name." I said I didn't know. I'd never been in a strip club before in my life, so it was odd that I walked into the wrong club on the right night. We were talking for a while and the next thing I knew, Tony was introducing me to the manager. The manager said he needed a bouncer, I said I needed a job, and the rest is history. I was a bouncer for strip clubs and music clubs for about twelve years, until I was about in my mid-30s. I had some pretty royal adventures!

When I worked for the strip clubs, the girls loved me. I was a big brother, a protector, and my intentions were to serve and protect, and make sure they didn't get hurt. My objective was to make people smile. I wasn't there to fight; I was there to keep people smiling. I never understood why some bouncers get an attitude because it's much easier to make people smile and help folks get along.

If someone was acting up, I'd walk over and say, "Hey, man, what's going on?" I'd be like a bulldozer operator and just sort of smooth out the bumps and make sure everyone calmed down. Life's too short, and it doesn't need to come to this or that. You don't need to end up getting charged by a police officer who's going to arrest you, and it's going to look really ugly if you have a girlfriend, or a wife, or a boss. I just talked sense to the guys that had an edge.

One day I was working at the club on 1st and Pike. I was at the cash register when a couple of these really tall dudes came in. They were really tall! Then a third really tall guy came in and I blurted out, "Holy smokes, you're Dennis Rodman!" and he said, "Whatever gave you that idea?" I said, "I play this basketball game on Sega every day, and I don't use anybody but you!" Dennis said, "Oh, really?"

Back in the day there was a video game we used to play; it was the Pistons against the Lakers on Sega, and me and my buddy Adam, and my best friend Scotty, would sit around and play video games all day. I'd play Rodman and he'd get 3-pointers from anywhere. Now here he was in front of me! It was really cool, and we ended up talking the whole time, and he never went inside to see the girls. I knew all about his career and I told him I appreciated the way he plays the games. Dennis plays with intensity and heart, and he hustles all the time, so we hit it off and he said, "Lo, do you need some tickets for the game?" and I said, "Sure!" Dennis gave me a couple of tickets and it was the first time I ever sat downstairs in the coliseum. This was before Key Arena. I had these great court-side seats and, holy smokes, it was awesome!

I was already a fan but this just made me appreciate the finer seats. I was migrating from upstairs and not really being into the game, to moving downstairs and sitting right next to the court. I was thinking, "Holy smokes! This is cool! They're 20 feet away from me!" It really opened up my vision about sports and how fortunate people really were, sitting as close as that to the action.

Not only was it a great game experience, but I also had post-game passes for afterward! I was able to go behind the scenes and hang out, waiting for the players to exit the locker room area. Dennis came out and said hi to me and everyone was wondering, "How the heck do you know him?" Dennis Rodman is really cool and was very nice to me; pretty much every time he came to town after that, if I needed tickets, I'd hit him up and it was no problem. Yes, he is flamboyant, but you know, at the same time, he's also genuine.

I knew which hotel he stayed in when he came to town, and back in the day most players would use false names when they registered. They didn't want people calling up the hotel and saying, "Yeah, hey, I need to leave a message for Michael Jordan..." so a lot of players had fake names. Dennis had a fake name and I'd call up and ask, "Is so-and-so staying at your hotel?" and they'd say, "Yes," and away we'd go!

When it comes to free tickets, there are players that have a lot of family in different towns, so they'll purchase extra tickets or hit up the other players on their team for the tickets they won't be using. Dennis didn't have any family or anybody special here in Seattle, so I was the lucky recipient pretty much every time he came to town, and this went on for several years. Thank you, Mr. Rodman!

As a bouncer, sometimes I'd score some really amazing gifts... but things weren't always so wonderful. There was a time I can never forget...

In 1990 there was a shooting that involved the club. It wasn't at the club; it was in a house behind the club where one of the girls lived. The club manager, Howard, was my friend and lived with me. He had moved out about a week before, and he'd also left the job at the club the day before the shooting. Howard was close friends with Autumn, one of the girls. Lance, her boyfriend, had come to me earlier in the evening and said he'd seen them kissing through the window of the little house behind the club where Howard had moved. Lance told me he felt he was going to do something stupid. That night he did some excessive drinking and then went back to his place and grabbed his roommate's gun. It was 2:00 in the morning when he came back and decided he was going to handle things, so he went into the little duplex and shot three people, then himself.

It was closing time and I was escorting Cricket, one of the girls, to her car. As we were walking across the parking lot I heard a garbled scream, like someone was screaming with liquid in their throat. I tried to figure out where the noise was coming from, and then I turned and saw the lights in the duplex. I told Cricket to get into her car and go as I turned and ran to the door of the building. I saw a silhouette through the curtain of the door, so I pushed the door open and there was Autumn, standing there, with blood trickling down each side of her face. The bullet had gone in through one side of her temple and out the other, and her eyes were bulging out of her head. I was looking at something out of a horror movie!

 My first instinct was to grab her hands, so I pulled her out and sat her down on the steps, and put my thumbs over the holes to stop the bleeding. At that moment Loren, our bartender, came running out of the club wondering what was going on because I was screaming, "Help! Somebody get help!" I was screaming at the top of my lungs and they heard me. "Get some towels!" I yelled, and Loren ran back and brought a bunch of towels. Then, from inside the house, I heard someone screaming, "Lo! Lo! Help me!" and I recognized Howard's voice, so I ran inside after Loren returned with towels and took Autumn. I didn't know what to expect.

I found Lance on the floor. He had shot himself, and the back of his head kind of went outward and you could see particles all over the place on the wall where he was lying. I grabbed his hand and he squeezed mine, and then it just went limp. I knew he was dead. Then I heard Howard groaning, "Forget him... forget him," so I turned toward Howard. He was on the couch, kind of leaning on his side, so I sat him up and about that time the blood started shooting out of his neck where he'd been shot. I was holding his neck trying to keep the blood in, and he said, "I need water...I need water..." So I went running for the kitchen to get him some water when I tripped over Kevin's legs. Kevin was one of our bartenders and he just happened to be over there, trying to be a good friend and keep the situation cool. He was lying in a pool of blood. I grabbed a glass of water and took it back to Howard. That's when my buddy Tony came in, and he went right to Kevin and held Kevin until Kevin passed.

I was losing my friends right in front of my eyes. That was one of the hardest nights of my life. I never planned on seeing any of my friends in this position, and here were four of my friends and they're all shot. It's one of those things you have to overcome. The first two paramedics who walked in both turned around and went out and threw up because it was such a gory scene. It's times like this that build character, and it was one of the nights in my life that opened my eyes to the realization that we're not here forever.

After that, I transferred to the downtown club because I just couldn't stand looking at that house. I couldn't deal with it. I moved downtown and within the first month I ended up getting stabbed!

At this other club, one of my jobs was to get soda from the storeroom, so I had to go out the door to the front of the club, then go down an alleyway, up another alleyway, and in through a back door where we kept the soda.

I was getting a couple of boxes one night, so I went down the alleys and into the storeroom. I grabbed the boxes and had one box up and over my left shoulder with the other one in my hand hanging down. I pushed open the door with my foot and as I turned to go down the alley, I suddenly felt something go thunk underneath my arm. There was a guy standing there and he had just stabbed me underneath my arm! I swung the box in my hand and slammed him with it as hard as I could. His buddy grabbed me but I shook him loose and then smashed him on the head with the other box!

I pulled the knife out and was standing over those two guys when two bicycle police officers were – boom – right there! They took control of the situation as I went to get help; my wound hurt and I knew I was bleeding. I got some towels from the club and stuck them under my arm and just kind of closed my armpit, hoping the bleeding would stop. I went to the hospital and ended up with six stitches.

To this day I don't know what they were doing. It was just my being in the wrong place at the wrong time. I had kicked the door open and I don't know if they were in the midst of something and got mad because the door suddenly opened. I never heard what happened to them.

I was also working downtown at the time of the Rodney King verdict. That was an incredibly dangerous night. It went from a normal night to chaos in one minute. I was outside the club when a cab driver pulled up and started yelling at me, "Hey, Big Boy, you better batten down the hatches. There's a big crowd coming down the street and they're not happy!" I ran to the corner and saw this crowd of over 200 people marching up the street. They were in front of the Improv, one of the comedy clubs, and all of a sudden I saw a car get rolled over!

I went running back to our club's door. There were people standing around the door and I started shouting and pushing everybody inside. Suddenly this crowd came around the corner running toward us, so to avoid a confrontation, my first instinct was to push everybody inside the building and shut the door. I started pulling the door shut and people on the other side were trying to keep it open! One hand had grabbed onto the edge of the door. It was a big metal door with the power of scissors...the hand wouldn't let go, and I kept pulling it closed as somebody on the other side was pulling it open. I knew it would be a disaster if the crowd on the street forced the door open so I kept pulling as hard as I could, and the door finally slammed shut, shearing off the tips of the fingers of that person's hand.

As I pulled the door shut, I had to keep pulling to keep it closed, and I was pulling on the inside and people on the street were pulling on the outside and I'm screaming, "Get the keys! Get the keys!" Finally my boss, Cal, brought the keys and we locked the door. People were banging on the glass but the glass on that door was really, really thick. It was a darkened door because it was a gentleman's club, so you couldn't see through it. We couldn't tell what was going on out there so I pulled on the Plexiglas that was on the inside of the door's window to see what was going on outside, and people were breaking windows across the street. It was just crazy mayhem!

About 10 minutes later a line of Seattle police officers in riot gear came marching down the street. I was relieved when they cleared the street, and that's when I opened the door and told the customers they could leave. Everybody was in a hurry to go, and the girls also wanted to leave because they were scared. I was walking one of the girls to her car and we had to go up through an alley. Out of the darkness came these gang members I knew, and suddenly I had a gun in my belly. One of the gangsters looked up at me and said, "You're lucky I know you, Big Man," and pulled the gun away and went running off. I know that the Lord was with me then.

There was an array of people downtown doing whatever they wanted. The tension down there was really thick for a couple of weeks. It was really bizarre.

Another time, at the club on 1st and Pike, I was standing out front talking with Jimmy, the front door guy, and we're just laughing and telling stories when several gang members came strolling along. All of a sudden a car goes rushing by and I heard, "Pop! Pop-pop-pop-pop-pop!" It sounded like a pan being hit with a ladle. The next thing I knew, I felt liquid running down my leg, and as I reached down and touched my leg, I realized I had been shot in my upper thigh! I thought, "What the hell?" I didn't feel any pain, but after I saw the blood on my hand, I thought, "Oh, man! Now I feel it!"

I was still pretty young, so none of these events, the shootings, the stabbing, the street riot, were enough to make me change my ways. I still liked traveling along the edge, and I continued drinking and smoking pot. I had had a few close calls, and shed a few of my nine lives, but I was young and this way of life suited me.

Because of my role as a club bouncer, I began to get a few gigs as part of the security team for different events. I began to meet a variety of different people and I was meeting celebrities. I was doing concert security for different bands, meeting band members, and meeting a number of actors and actresses. I did security for Richard Karn, whose TV name was Al Borland, the costar on Home Improvement. Richard Karn was hosting Star Days, a Seattle comedy event that lasted for about three years. Star Days held charity basketball games, charity softball games, and celebrity golf tournaments; periodically they also held a gala event in which regular people would get dressed up in nice evening clothes and rub elbows with celebrities and stars. It was pretty popular.

I was doing security at a golf tournament when I met Samuel L. Jackson. He had sliced a ball a couple of times and I called out, "C'mon Sam! Hit 'em straight!" I was just being a smart aleck, but he turned and looked at me and said, "Well, who are you, Bubba?" I said, "Come on, man, you gotta hit this one straight. It's gonna launch and it's gonna be beautiful!" This was when he was on the driving range, and after I said that, he hit three balls really far, and really straight, all right in a row. He was surprised and said, "Hey! Why don't you come hang out with me on the course?" I had become his good luck charm and his luck held for six holes. On the seventh hole, he hooked it, and he hooked it bad, so he said, "Okay, Bubba, you're done. Get outta here." So I said okay and left.

I took off and walked around, checking out some of the other golfers. I saw him a couple of holes later and I said, "Sam, how's your game?" and he said, "We're doing good, Bubba, we're doing all right. You want to hang out with me some more?" and I said, "Sure!" I stayed on course with him for a few more holes, and once he had finished, everyone went to the club house.

In the club house, the stars and guests were sitting around talking, and I ended up pulling up a chair and sitting and talking with Samuel L. Jackson. He is one of the coolest people I have ever met in my entire life. We hit it off, and he asked me to walk the red carpet with him at the opening of Seattle's Planet Hollywood, July 1996, which was one of the most incredible experiences of my life. I got hold of my sister Marlee and my niece Britnee and said, "Hey, I've got tickets to this event. Let's go!" We ended up walking the red carpet with Samuel L. Jackson at the opening of Planet Hollywood. It was just an amazing event, rubbing elbows and meeting people, and we all had a really great time.

A Day in the Life

On a regular day, I wake up in the morning, and my day depends on what's going on for Dad. I like to check on him first thing and make sure he's still breathing! Then it's usually time for a shower and shine to get all the funk off. I usually read the morning sports to see what's going on in the sports world, and then I check out the rest of the paper. I look at the obituaries to see if my name is in there.

You might laugh, but I'll never forget the time when I was 19 years old and there was a rumor going around that I'd passed away. I'd heard there was a teacher at my old high school who said she'd been to my funeral! I thought it would be funny to walk into her class out of the blue...and she turned as white as a ghost! It was funny because it was like, what the heck? After that I always thought you can die without dying, which is kind of weird.

After I read the papers, I check to see what's on the list for breakfast. I usually have cereal with a sliced-up banana. I don't drink coffee because I want to be a big guy, not a little guy! I love iced tea but not first thing in the morning. When Dad wakes up late, I make sure that things are worked out for him. Dad likes his doughnut and banana for breakfast every day.

My dad's 82 and he's got neuropathy in his feet really bad, so he doesn't walk around a lot, and there are times you have to keep your eye on him.

Some mornings I start my day at the gym. 3:30 a.m. comes early! The gym opens up at 4 a.m., and I start my gym routine with 15 to 20 minutes on the bike, and then I do a stretchy band workout where I'm pulling and stretching on the bands to get the muscles moving. Until I get my shoulder surgery, it's kind of hard on the shoulders. There's a lot of pain, but I've learned to work through it. Life's not going to stop for you, so you have to keep on keeping on!

The gym is pretty busy early in the morning. There are Zumba classes and spinning classes, and some people doing weights. I usually do about a 70-minute workout, sometimes longer, depending on what I'm feeling. For the most part, my workout is focused on cardio. The elliptical machine is hard on my knees, but at the same time it's one of those things you have to push through even though it hurts a bit. When I started the elliptical I could only do about a minute or two. I couldn't see how people could go as long as they do, because some people go 30, 40, or 50 minutes to an hour, and I think, man, that is awesome! One day I hope to get there, but right now I can do about 10 to 12 minutes. That's the thing; start down the path and keep at it because you'll get better and better as you go.

When my workout is done, I cruise home and shower right away; I might even go back to sleep for an hour or so. On gym mornings my breakfast will be a bowl of oatmeal and some egg whites because that gives me the energy I need, and it replenishes what I put out in the gym. If you want a good start to your day, you have to start it right with a good breakfast. Yes, I fry my egg whites...I'm not Rocky Stallone yet!

After my dad gets going, I usually run some errands like everybody else. Some days I volunteer at a school and read to the kids, or I'll play with them on the playground. I love to be around kids, and I love to make them smile. I try to build them up and let them know the future isn't as hard as some people make it seem.

I've been invited by several schools, but the one I go to the most is Wildwood Elementary School out in Federal Way. There's a fourth grade teacher there, Ms. Ta Sukovaty, and she asks me to come out and read to the kids once in a while. On other days, other teachers ask me to come and talk to the kids. Hanging out with the kids, reading and playing with them... Well, it's one of the most special feelings you can imagine.

Sometimes Dad and I will go on an adventure. I'll drive us up into the hills and we'll explore old logging roads. We've spent a lot of cool times together just go, go, going. There's so much to this beautiful country that God made, and Dad and I will drive down around Mt. Saint Helens, Mt. Adams, or do the 101 loop out to Aberdeen and around Forks and back to Port Angeles, coming home on the ferry. Some days we end up at Mt. Baker, and some days we just go where the jeep takes us. We have a lot of fun on our adventures and it's one of the things that have really helped me and my dad become close. There's just us, and he'll tell me all these stories about, "Oh, yeah, I remember when I did this...or when I did that." Since he did a lot of bulldozer work, sometimes we'll drive past the place and he'll say, "I remember when I bulldozed that!" Being with my dad and hearing all his stories gives me a lot of food for thought. It's always fun hanging out with Pops.

Something else I do which is a whole lot of fun, is marketing for Jacknut Apparel. They have a sportswear line with shirts, jackets, hats, and other stuff. They came to me years ago and asked if I'd wear a T-shirt with Jacknut Apparel on it; I told them to give me a month and I'd make them famous, and I think it took about three weeks. My buddy, Eric Gardner, introduced me to Christian, the owner. Christian offered to make some custom shirts, and I was thinking that it would be really cool. It's hard to find shirts in my size.

The major league teams don't market to the big fans, and it's terrible because there are fans out there who are big kids, so it's not fair that everybody else gets to wear all this cool gear and the big kids don't. So I suggested to Christian that his company start making big sizes for big people. Some of my friends were ecstatic because they're big guys, or big girls, and now they can also buy shirts that are cool. The gear doesn't have the franchise logo on them, but the designs are close enough so that big kids and adults can have something cool to wear.

We started out with a couple of shirts. One was for T. J. Houshmandzadeh. He was a wide receiver for the Seahawks after eight years with the Bengals. We thought the design was pretty catchy! It was, "Housh, there it is!" That became pretty popular and we had some good sales.

The second shirt we made was for Owen Schmitt, the Seahawk fullback. Owen was with us for two seasons before he went over to the Eagles. His shirt said, "Schmitt happens!" About a week later we were at the game and Owen came running out and bashed his helmet on his forehead. All of a sudden the blood came running down his face and there was a really good picture of it; we put the picture on a T-shirt and marketed it as "Get Schmitt-faced." That shirt sold like hot cakes, it was incredible! Owen went to West Virginia University, so everybody there wanted one of these shirts, and we were shipping them all over the globe. We had orders from Australia, London, and everywhere. Jacknut's website went from a few hits a day to over 50,000 in just a few days. That was really cool!

We can't sell it anymore. The NFL attorney came after us and gave us a cease and desist order. They didn't realize it was going to sell so well, so they shut it down when they found out. Now it's a collector's item! I happen to have a few of them...

Well, back to my day in the life...I like to cook so I usually make Dad a good meal for dinner, or my best friend, Scotty, and I go out and eat somewhere and bring something good back for Dad.

Dad loves pasta, it's his favorite. He loves spaghetti and meatballs, and he loves macaroni and cheese...but you have to make the mac and cheese from scratch, like Marlee does, not from a box. Dad also loves Pho...he goes nuts for noodle soup.

In the evening Dad and I will watch some TV. We have our shows. We like Pawn Stars, Ax Men, Ice Road Truckers, and Moonshiners. TV is a good way to spend some time together because we talk during the show and enjoy each other's company. Before long, it's time for bed. I'll make sure the cats are inside so the raccoons don't get them, and then I lock everything up and shut off all the lights...and it's dream time.

Winning the Lottery

Some people know I won the lottery back in 1998, but most people don't know the money went out as fast as it came in. Not because I was careless with the money, but because, along with my being generous to my family, something disastrous happened to me. Here's that story.

Dad always bought five Lotto and five Quinto tickets every Wednesday and every Saturday. His thinking was that someday he would win, and all he had to do was buy tickets steadily because you can't win if you don't play. In 1998, the lottery was twice a week. Because dad was so convinced that he was going to win, I started doing the same thing. Every week we'd each spend $20 buying lottery tickets. We always said that no matter who won, we would split the money with the family. We bought a lot of tickets that didn't win!

In mid-January, 1999, I was watching the news while making dinner, and I heard something about the December 31st Quinto drawing going unclaimed.

I hadn't been checking my tickets like I usually did, so I had a small stack of them. Of course, I'd bought tickets for that drawing so I grabbed my stack and found the two for that day. I looked at the first one, and nope – no winner. I looked at the second one, and I looked at the numbers I'd written down – looked at the ticket – looked at the numbers – looked at the ticket – looked at the numbers – looked at the ticket, and I realized, "Wow, all these numbers match!" I started thinking, "That's impossible!"

I checked it about a dozen times and then it began to sink in. It hit me like a ton of bricks and I was the most excited person in the world! The prize was good, more money than I could ever imagine.

I went running into my roommate's room yelling, "We won! We won!" I was screaming, jumping around in jubilation with Adam, and I picked him up and began squeezing him in this giant bear hug until he yelled, "Let me go! You're hurting me!" So I sat him down, and holy smokes, I immediately began thinking, "What am I going to do, what am I going to do?"

My first reaction was to call my dad...and Dad drove from Sumner to Burien in less than 20 minutes! When he got to my house, we sat down at the kitchen table and we talked about it. We decided to do what we'd always decided to do, and that was to split up the money among the family.

The first thing I did with my share of the money was I went and bought a headstone for my mother. Then I paid off my debts, and bought season tickets to the Seahawks and the Sonics; I also bought a Jeep to replace my old Scout I was driving. I still had a lot of money left over...but that's when my nightmares started because I ended up in the hospital with flesh-eating bacteria just three months later, and the hospital bills cost $127,000. My jubilation with winning the lottery was quickly over. I was cleaned out, but I thank God I had the money to pay all the medical bills.

The part that made it so hard for me was the greed I witnessed. People were coming out of the woodwork asking me for money, not knowing that the money had been divided up and distributed. My share wasn't that much, and I needed it for myself, and it all wound up going for hospital bills. Family and friends I hadn't seen or talked to in years found me and asked me to loan them $5,000 for this and $15,000 for that; they wanted to start a business, they wanted me to invest in something they had going on, they had bills they were hoping I would pay...it was very hard to say no to these people because they thought I had so much. I've never liked refusing people anything, so this was a very painful experience. My suggestion to people who want to win money or play the lottery: don't buy the tickets. It's not all it's cracked up to be. It's better to avoid the whole thing than go through what I did!

When I won the lottery, I told Jim McIlvaine; he was playing for the Sonics at that time. He immediately took me under his wing and introduced me to his investment advisor. We invested the money right away, so that was a good thing, and I would've been set for life if I'd stayed with the financial plan, but it wasn't long before I was hospitalized. I didn't have insurance because I wasn't working at the time, and there was no other way I could pay for all the medical expenses. I had just won the lottery, so I felt invincible...but the Lord had another path for me to follow.

My advice to anyone who has won the lottery is to immediately select an experienced financial investment advisor and get that money securely and safely invested. Call me up and let me know, because I know a really good advisor. Get that money into the hands of somebody who knows how to protect your windfall because it just goes so fast. It's so easy to lose it all.

Battling Flesh-Eating Parasites

I noticed I had what I thought was an ingrown hair near my groin, and it was a bump the size of a peanut. Over the next four or five days that bump grew from the size of a peanut to the size of a lime to the size of a lemon to the size of an orange to the size of a grapefruit.

On the fifth day I woke up and knew I had to do something because it was really hurting. I also had cold and flu symptoms and I felt terrible. It hurt to walk because this growth had become so big and painful. Foolishly, I was trying to find a way to pop the head of this thing, and finally, I remember it was Sunday morning, and I got it to pop, and the smell was horrible! It was horrific and it smelled like death! My buddy, Adam, who lived upstairs, ran me over to the emergency room at Riverton Hospital. The doctors looked at it but had no idea what it could be. They put me in an ambulance and shipped me downtown to Harborview Medical Center.

Harborview's emergency room staff was phenomenal! They took care of me right away and in a few minutes there was a room full of doctors looking at my groin. I admit that was kind of weird, and it was very scary, too. When doctors are looking at a gigantic growth on your groin and aren't sure what it is, let me tell you, it's frightening!

I had never really been in a hospital before either, because I've never been that sick, but here I was, and I was freaking out because I didn't know what was happening to me. Nobody I knew was with me because Adam wasn't allowed to ride in the ambulance. While I was waiting in the exam room, I heard the doctors say they needed to get me into surgery right away.

As they were wheeling me down the hall, I felt so empty. I was afraid because I was by myself, with no one standing by me. I felt so awful. And then, as my bed was rolling down the corridor,

I heard familiar voices! It was my friend, Kelly, and his wife Susie. How they made it to the hospital so quickly was beyond me, but they were right there when I needed them most. Kelly grabbed my hand, and he said, "Bro, you're going to make it through this okay. I love you. You're my buddy." And right then I felt such incredible comfort. Even if I was going to die, I was ready because I knew that people cared about me. Then, when I was waiting in the pre-op area, the nurse at the desk brought me a phone; my sister Marlee was calling. I talked to her, and she is a God-loving woman, and she said, "Lo, don't you dare accept any of this...you're going to be fine...God's going to get you through this." I felt reassured by Marlee's words and by her love, and I felt more steady.

About then, I heard one doctor quietly say to another that he didn't think I was going to live through this. I started thinking again, "If I die, it is what it is. I'll be okay either way." That's when I found peace and I was at ease with what was going on. When I finished talking with my sister, I passed out. The pain was so intense with the infection running through my body the way it was. I must've come to briefly, because I remember the lights and all the fuss that was going on around me. But then there was a different Light...and I remember it was a brilliant Light. I saw people around me that I knew had passed away. My Aunt Sherrie appeared; she was a big part of my younger life. It seemed like she was shaking her head, like "No, go back..." I don't remember it all, because it was like a dream, but I remember it was a weird feeling inside. Seeing the Light and wondering what I was experiencing, I really didn't know if I was alive or dead.

The next thing I remember was waking up in the post-op room and gagging because I had a tube stuck down my throat to clean out all the junk. I also remember I feeling frustrated because I couldn't move. Apparently I had been strapped to the bed since I had been moving so much during surgery, trying to stay alive. The surgeon came to see me and he said, "I just want to let you know you're a fighter. You made that surgery so much easier for us than it would have been. In fact, we lost you three times on the table."

I was devastated, I was in tears, I didn't know what was going on. My family was there with me. I don't remember a whole lot, but I know I was in intensive care for eight days. During the first five days I went through three more surgeries, and every day they had to change the dressing on the wound two or three times.

They had this medical technique called water-picking in which water is sprayed into the wound to try to get all the dead tissue out. My time in the hospital was quite an experience, especially because no one had ever seen an affliction like mine before, and I didn't know what was going to happen next, or if I'd even leave the hospital. I was very depressed. Everything had been going so well, and then all of a sudden this darkness had descended on me.

I kept thinking, "Why don't they just let me die? I don't want to be here anymore." I didn't know how long my medical condition was going to take to heal. The doctors told me on the eleventh day that I'd be in the hospital another two or maybe even four more months, and I'd probably require another five or six surgeries.

Marlee said I didn't need to let that happen. She said it was the Darkness working through those surgeons and that she would help me dispel the negative energy. The next day her boyfriend, Val, visited me and laid hands on me, and spoke tongues on me, and prayed over me, and I felt the Spirit of Christ moving through my body. When people talk about feeling Christ, I'm the guy that really, truly felt Christ, and I felt Him moving through my body in such a way that it warmed me.

That night I slept well for the first time since I'd been in the hospital. I told the nurses to take me off the pain medications because I just didn't like the way the drugs made me feel; on my first night off the pain meds I actually slept. I woke up the next morning, sat up on my bed, stood up, and pulled my little IV bags and all the little buttons and buzzers and bells that were hooked to it...I had two different IV lines in me, one in my neck and one in my arm...and I started walking. I made myself get up and I started walking down the hallway. The nurses were all looking at me like I was crazy and they said, "Um, Lorin, what are you doing?" I said, "I feel great, I'm ready to go home!" They were looking at me like, "Uh oh! You shouldn't be doing that! How are you able to get up and walk around?"

So I'm walking around the hall and I said, "I have to do two laps, and then I'll get back in bed." They were saying, "No, no, no...! You need to get back into bed right now!" I was adamant and I said, "NO." I told them I was going to walk two laps around the corridor. They trailed behind me, and I did my two laps, and when I was done, I went back to my room and got into bed. I felt human again and like my old self, happy once more. I have always been such a happy-go-lucky guy, and yet here I'd been, going through this depression and darkness. I had started to believe I wasn't going to come out of it, but because of the feeling and healing of Christ moving through me, I had been turned around. The nurses and doctors were talking to me and asking if I was okay, and I told them I felt better than I'd felt in a long time! It was great to start feeling better again!

Later that day there were 13 doctors in the room. Some were interns, but about eight of the doctors were involved in my case, trying to figure out what I had and what to do about it. At the time, I was the third case of necrotizing fasciitis in Washington State, and during the time I was in the hospital, another eight cases of this disease had been recognized, making 11 total. Some of the other people's cases were even worse than mine.

On the same day I insisted on doing two laps around the

corridor, these 13 doctors were in my room. My wound was unwrapped and they looked at it, and they had very puzzled looks on their faces. One doctor said, "Oh, my God!" I said, "What? What?" I instantly started worrying again. The doctor looked at me in disbelief and he said the infection was gone and the color was back!

At the top of my lungs I bellowed out, "HALLELUJAH!!"

The doctors were looking at me like, "Whoa!" and I said, "Jesus healed me!"

They looked at me funny and puzzled, but I knew…I know the power of Christ. I know what I went through and I know what I experienced, and that was one of the most incredible moments of my life!

Dr. Engrov said, "Well, as long as you don't have any cold or flu-like symptoms over the next three to four days," he says, "we're going to take you off the antibiotics, and if you don't have any cold or flu-like symptoms over the next few days after that, we'll send you home. I said, "Send me home today, I'm ready!" Well, I still had a big wound in my groin and they were pondering how to fix that, so I wasn't going home that day. But I was going home soon!

During the time I had been in the hospital, Hersey Hawkins from the Sonics visited me, and Hersey brought Charles Barkley with him. Jim McIlvaine, the Sonics center, also stopped by. The Sonics sent me flowers and cards, and my friends Kelly and Susie had a big card that had been signed by Gary Peyton and the whole Sonics team, and all these people and encouragements had helped me get through this ordeal. At first I didn't understand, but after my amazing experience of how God moves through us, and how Christ can move through our bodies and heal us, it was an immense eye-opener that inspired me toward wanting to go on with life and contribute to the lives of others.

For the next ten months my sisters, Marlee and Bonnie, were my home nurses, and they had to change the wound's dressing several times a day; it's pretty amazing to experience the regrowth of tissue in the body. I felt so humble because I couldn't do this on my own. There was no way I could have changed the bandages and done all the other things that needed to get done because I was an invalid. Every day I thank the Lord for my sisters because they sure took good care of me!

About nine years later, in 2008, I had another run in with necrotizing fasciitis. I was coaching my kids in a Little League game, and I was standing at third base, shivering. I started to get chilled, and I felt these cold and flu-like symptoms coming on again. I knew my legs were bad because they were purple, so I knew something was going on but I didn't know what. I went into the dugout to fire up the kids but I just didn't have the gumption. I was starting to fade pretty quickly. One of the moms came over and she said, "Big Lo, you need to take it easy," and I said, "I'm freezing...I'm freezing," so she wrapped a sleeping bag around me and all the parents were telling me I should go see a doctor right away. I said, "Oh, no, I'll be fine. I've just got to go home and put my legs up and relax, and I'll be fine." That night, at the house, I began to feel sicker and sicker throughout the night, and finally in the middle of the night, I drove over to Highline Hospital's emergency room.

When the doctors saw me, they said I had venous stasis, which is a condition of slow blood in the veins. They gave me some antibiotics and told me to go home. They said I'd feel better in four to ten days. Of course, I trusted them, so I took the antibiotics and went home. Two days later I ended up in emergency surgery at Harborview Hospital. Now I had five abscesses in my leg that had ulcerated from diabetes complications. The doctor told me I was diabetic and I either had to lose weight, or die. I weighed over 650 pounds. I had brought myself to the point of death again.

I had surgery on my legs because of the five abscesses, and one of them was really big, so they had to carve into my leg. The doctor said this particular wound had turned into necrotizing fasciitis, the flesh-eating bacteria. "Oh, my God!" I thought. "Here I go again."

I was very weak in my left leg because now I had all these holes cut into it, and I had to have the bandages on the wounds changed twice a day. I was in the hospital again, this time for 14 days. Once again, I knew I had to get up out of bed and move. I had to teach myself to walk again because my left leg had almost no power. It took me a couple of days to get the gumption to want to get up and do this. I relied a lot on the Lord, on prayer, and a lot of good people who stayed by my side. My whole family had been there every time for me, Marlee and Bonnie, and Dad. My niece and nephews also kept me going. It was another really tough moment, but I was blessed and I got through it. This is another experience that helped shape me.

A year later I had to have surgery to straighten out my toes. I was in Highline Hospital again for this one, and this time I contracted MRSA, a staph infection that you sometimes get when you're in the hospital. I was in the hospital for nine days battling this situation.

In 2010, my gall bladder acted up and the doctors wanted to do a simple gallbladder removal. The surgeon accidentally poked holes in my bile tubes so my kidneys shut down, my liver shut down, and I flatlined again.

Subconsciously I heard the doctor say, "He's gone." But I wasn't going to let that happen! I started jerking and moving on the bed saying, "No, I'm not! No, I'm not!" The doctors were shocked!

I was then sent to Virginia Mason to get a stint put on the bile tubes to close the holes the surgeons had poked into them. While I was there, the bandages on my staples, where they had cut me open for the gall bladder removal, were never changed. I was in Virginia Mason for seven days and the whole time I was there, the medical staff never changed the dressing. Thank God that Tonie Peckham stayed with me while I was there. She made things much more comfortable.

Once I was back home, I wasn't feeling good so I went to the doctor and had him check the wound, and he peeled off the dressing and he said, "Well, didn't you change the bandages?" looking at me like I was supposed to do that, like I was the doctor or nurse. I got really upset and angry with him. Then he started snipping the staples and once again I smelled that dead flesh smell. "Oh, what's that?" I said, but I knew what it was before he told me. He looked at it and said, "It looks like necrotizing fasciitis!"

Now I had to go into surgery again, and they had to clean out the wound. This time they couldn't staple it closed because there was so much dead tissue, and once again I had to have multiple daily bandage changes.

Once again it was my sister to the rescue. Home nurses had come in to do some of the changes but it was mostly Bonnie, my sister, who did the bulk of the nursing. My other sister, Marlee, had moved out of state by then. Have I told you how much I love my sisters? Well, listen up! It's thanks to them and my dad that I was able to live through these miserable experiences.

There's one more health story to relate. In 2012, I was at Seafair watching the hydroplane races. I knew I had a sore on the back of my leg, and I didn't really know what it was, but I was on an antibiotic. I wasn't supposed to be in the sun, but I didn't know that because I hadn't read all the literature that had come with the drug. The next thing I knew, I had a really bad sunburn. It was over 90° and I was out in direct sunlight. I was getting burned to a crisp. My face was burned, my arms were burned, and my legs were burned. I put some lotion on, but I was also pushing myself because I had an Internet TV show and I was getting a lot of good stories for it. I went back the second day and soaked up some more sun, and I went back the third day and it was just as bright and hot as ever.

On the third day, an older gentleman came up to me and he said, "Excuse me, son, but I think you're bleeding from the back of your leg." I'd been wearing compression stockings so I hadn't felt or seen anything, but when I look down, there was blood all over the back of my leg. It turned out I had an abscess on the back of my leg that I didn't know was an abscess, and it had exploded. I had to leave immediately and check into the hospital. Once again I had those cold and flu-type symptoms... and the medical staff had to clean out the wound thoroughly because they didn't want it to get to the necrotizing fasciitis stages. They drained the wound on my leg, and once again I had a leg that had to be bandaged. This was the last big medical event that happened to me, and I pray that I am done with flesh-eating parasites and abscesses forever!

Hey! Coach!

Before I can tell the story of my coaching career, I have to tell you that I got in trouble for selling pot. Having been an avid smoker, I told several people that if I ever got in trouble for smoking pot or being around it, I'd quit. The weekend after I got in trouble, I went hunting with my cousin Rick, and we stayed up in the mountains for almost a week so I could get away from pot once and for all. I knew that the best way for me to quit was to go cold turkey and just stop.

One of the hardest things to do is to quitting drugs or alcohol, and smoking or overeating. It's so hard to do unless your mind is set, and unless your body is set to let it go for good, and I got my mind and my body right by being up in the woods, sitting around a campfire with my dad and other family members. It was a peaceful time for me, and that helped me open my eyes to see I needed to find something else, I needed to start a new chapter.

Thinking about what I could do that would keep me busy, out of trouble, and distract me from temptation, I went to my niece's and nephew's school. They needed an after-school program coordinator for flag football. That seemed like just the thing, so I said I'd do that, and I starting coaching. That's when I discovered how much fun it was hanging out with these kids! These kids needed something to do after school. They needed to have a positive experience that kept them focused on their school work and on completing their education.

I always tried to keep my focus on the kids, and I told them not to drink or do drugs because there's just no place for that in an active and healthy life. Drinking and drugging slows you down, puts up obstacles that are difficult to navigate, and it also helps a person procrastinate and lose time and energy. This afterschool program was at McClure Middle School on Queen Anne Hill, and I met dozens and dozens of neat kids. After a few seasons there, I went from McClure to Madison Middle School in West Seattle.

I met many kids from broken homes, and kids who were struggling with all kinds of difficult situations. Some kids were living with their grandma because both their mom and dad were in prison. Some families had almost no money and were struggling to pay the bills and put food on the table. Some kids had alcoholic parents, and others were living with parents who were handicapped and relied on their child too much. There were so many different things these kids were going through... and then there were also the kids from wealthy families who had everything on a silver platter. It was astonishing to see this mix of all types of kids. On top of that, it was interesting to see the different ethnic backgrounds of all these kids. Schools today have diverse populations, so I was seeing a wide variety of kids with different perspectives and attitudes toward life, and it made me realize how much change has been happening in our cities and in our country.

I wanted the kids' respect, and I wanted them to avoid doing the stupid things I had done like smoking weed and drinking. I wanted to make things better for these kids, and I did everything I could. I taught them to be respectful of each other and of the teams we played, I taught them how to be a good sport, and how to be a good team member, and how to support each other...I encouraged them to do well in school, to ask questions in class if they didn't know something, to go out of their way to help somebody who was struggling or in trouble, and I coached them to build good character in themselves and support good character in others. I wasn't just their football coach; I became their behavior and life coach as well as their friend.

Eventually, I wanted to move up and coach junior football. These were the 12 to 14-year-old athletes. I wanted this level because this was the most vulnerable age, when kids were starting to get into trouble. I did the same thing with Little League baseball and was able to position myself so I could coach the 12 to 14-year-olds. I learned from them as much as they learned from me. Every good teacher, coach, and parent knows this is true. That's how I felt because I was learning so much about life and how to get along with all the diverse influences I was exposed to with these kids. I really wanted to be known as a nice and helpful person and not the jerk I had been when I was a bouncer at the clubs. Here I was, in front of all these impressionable kids, kids who could benefit from what I had to offer, and it felt like I was up on a stage, trying to show them right from wrong and how to be better human beings. I've heard it said that the best student in the class is the teacher, and now I understand.

That was one of the toughest things to learn: how to teach kids right from wrong. Every coach has to make a choice between either being their buddy, and swearing and having a good time and making fun of things, or setting an example by watching your language and modeling good behavior and right action. Some coaches go out drinking after they coach the kids. When I was working at Bleachers Pub, I saw a lot of high school coaches come in and get drunk after practice; I remember thinking, "Well, that's not really good, but to each his own." Now that I was a coach, I realized that good behavior and good character is always important. How can we make any progress as a society if the people who work with our kids don't model good behavior?

When I was coaching junior football for the Interbay Eagles, I found a love for the game that I had lost during my years as a bouncer and hanging out with the crowd that hung around the bar scene. I had lost my focus and my vision on what I wanted, and why. I quickly realized that I wanted to win a championship for the kids I was working with. I wanted to teach them how to win, and I started out as the assistant coach for the Interbay Eagles. Our coach, Ron West, was a really neat guy, and I also coached with a guy named Shane Toupal and Jerry Wolf; we had great camaraderie, and we did a really good job coaching the kids. It was only our first year so we had our ups and downs, but we did fairly well.

The next year Ron had an opportunity to go to the high school level so Shane and Jerry nominated me to be the coach. Great! But now what should I do? I started thinking about football from a new perspective and I designed my own plays, and an entire scheme of how to run a team. In our first year we made it all the way to the championship game with the Silverlake Timberwolves and our kids played their butts off. It was a cold and stormy day with the rain coming down sideways. One of my favorite kids, Kaosio Saeteurn, came up to me and said, "Coach, I can't feel my balls!" We lost the game but we had so much fun!

The kids were honest with me. They were all about having fun and I helped make it that way and tried to teach them this is what it's all about...all of us getting together and doing our best, and having fun doing it, so coaching for me was a great joy.

I coached Queen Anne Little League for the better part of eight years, and I watched all these kids grow up; now they're adults and it's so cool to see how some of them matured and owned their success. One kid I coached early on was KeiVarae Russell and he's the starting corner back for the Notre Dame Irish. It's quite an honor to see that, you know. It's amazing to know that someone I coached has reached that level. I hope he goes to the pros because he's one kid who can.

My kids and I never got to win a championship, but we played in two of them. In one championship game we lost to the Timberwolves; they were a big team and had more depth than we did, but we earned the right to face them! The next year, the NW Junior Football League decided to set a weight restriction of 160 pounds for 14-year olds. Well, if you can't recruit a line of 14-year olds that are bigger than 160 pounds, you're hurting. I was looking for those huge 13-year olds that are 225 pounds in the Queen Anne and Magnolia neighborhoods, but I just didn't have kids that size. Still, with the Interbay team, we won a tournament championship, and that was a huge triumph for my kids.

I know I made a positive impact on lots of those kids because I still get phone calls from some of them today, and that's a special part of my life. I get emails, Facebook messages, and Twitter posts from kids I've coached. I've had several kids send me private messages thanking me for everything I taught them, and it feels so good, you just can't imagine!

I even got a job once because of my coaching. Shane, the fellow I coached with, owned Bleachers Pub, the sports bar. I was hurting one time and needed cash and Shane came up and said, "I know you need a job. Why don't you come and bartend for me?" I said, "Bartend? I don't drink," and he said, "That's a perfect reason for you to come bartend for me!" So I went to Bleachers Pub and worked for him for about five years, and it was a really great time working for Shane with so many sports activities happening all the time. It was a lot of fun. I enjoy meeting new people and making new friends, and it's been a great satisfaction for me.

My coaching stopped abruptly in 2008 because that's when I had the surgery. I had to quit then, but it's a part of my life I'll always treasure.

We Are Sea-Fence!™

In 2002 we were blessed with a new stadium, Seahawks Stadium, and I was talking to my buddy Charlie one day, and he said, "You know, you really have to switch it up now. Everybody's got a D-Fence sign, so with our having a new stadium, you have to go to a new level." I said, "There's not really anything I can go with..." and he looked at the Seattle Seahawk logo and said, "Well, what about Sea-Fence™?", and I said, "Sea-Fence™? What's your logic behind Sea-Fence™?"

Charlie said, "Well, look, our defense is on the field and our Seafence is in the stands. There is nothing more powerful than the sea!"

That's when it clicked, and it was just the perfect thing! People ask me all the time, "What's Sea-Fence™ all about? I don't get it." But to me, it makes perfectly good sense if you look at it. A lot of people like the 12th Man, and a lot of people like the idea of fans supporting their team. For me, Sea-Fence™ became a metaphor for our Seattle fans. We used to do the Wave, and that was a very powerful fan activity, but the Wave is gone now because during the game everybody's already standing up. Even though we lost the Wave, and it's kind of a bummer, this is where the Sea-Fence™ comes in. WE are the power, WE are the energy!

During the first two years at Seahawks Stadium, we didn't have any rain. It didn't rain for a single home game, and that was really weird because it was almost like rain was forbidden on game days. Then when the stadium name changed from Seahawks Stadium to Qwest Field in 2004, we started getting downpours! When the name changed to CenturyLink, we started to get snow, sleet, hail, and lightning! It made me think about ways to make a stronger sign, one that can stand up to the crazy weather.

I'd been making the Sea-Fence™ sign from foam-core, and it's a lot better than cardboard, but it still gets sloppy when it gets wet. I found some plastic stuff that I could work with, but then I met this guy named Scott Davis. Scott owns the Davis Sign Company, and I thank my lucky stars for him. He and his company started making my Sea-Fence™ signs, and I asked the Seahawks for permission to put the Seahawks logo on the fence and they said I could. This has developed into a kind of team effort. It was so nice to have a fence that was actually sturdy and I didn't have to worry about in the rain. It's made out of plastic now, and it was really great to meet Scott and get the Davis Sign Company on board making the signs. Without them, I know I would've become really tired of the soaking wet foam-core that rips apart when it gets wet, and boy, do they rip! Nowadays I've been getting my signs through the folks at Diecutstickers.com.

A few people have tried to emulate me, and I love that. There's a guy and a girl that dressed up as me for Halloween...the guy came as a Super Fan action figure last year, and he was Big Lo with the Sea and the Fence signs; and the girl dressed up as a puffy foam finger. That was pretty cool! Another time there was this little kid with a Sea-Fence™ sign, and I met him and he said he wants to be Big Lo when he grows up. I took a picture of him; he was a cute little kid.

Lately my shoulders have been hurting from smacking the signs. I don't just hold the sign up; I smack the sign to add a little spark for the guys. It's funny because when I'm too quiet, they look at me now like, "Okay, are you going to start smacking that thing or what?" Also, my shoulders take a beating during the games as people jump up on me and smack my shoulders in celebration, and Rob in Row 2 has actually stopped hitting me on my shoulders! My feet get sore from standing on them as long as I do at the games, so that's why I take ibuprofen. I'm ready to do a commercial for Advil, or maybe Aleve! Call me...

My Own Action Figure!

After Les Carpenter's big story in the Seattle Times in 2005, there seemed to be a buzz in the air of different ways people imagined using my likeness, and me. A company called Accoutrements in Mukilteo came to me and said they wanted to do a fan-based action figure and they wanted to use my image. Their inquiry came by email, asking if I'd be interested.

I called them right away and said I'd absolutely love to see what we can do about this. My first question was whether I would get paid, and they said yes. I said, "Where do I sign?" I drove up to Mukilteo and I met with Mark Pahlow, the owner and CEO of Archie McPhee. Mark told me what they wanted to do and introduced me to a few of the guys who worked there. They explained how the process works. They were going to take pictures of me, and do different articulations of how my arms and legs move, and then convert those into diagrams that could be used to create a five or six-inch 3D plastic representation of me.

I then met with the marketing team about color schemes and what colors they thought would work best, and I stressed that the Seahawks colors were the way to go. I told them the Seahawks were going to win the Super Bowl this year, but they told me they preferred the Sonics because the Sonics were on a roll. They felt the Sonics were having a really good season in 2005, and they wanted to use Sonics colors. I said, "Well, we'll see how that goes...but personally I'd rather market to 66,000 fans rather than just 16,000." But, what did I know? They decided to go with the Sonics colors.

On the action figure, I'm wearing my iconic number 23 jersey. It isn't really a jersey, but a Carleton designer shirt I found in a store that sells clothing for big people. It just happened to have the Sonics colors, and I thought, "Wow!" Anytime I find something in my size, it's exciting! ...and in the Sonics colors no less!

The Accoutrements team then created the action figure designs, did whatever magic they do, and sent the information to China. I guess the Chinese factory managers and the Accoutrements team worked out all the details and finally the action figure was approved and mass-produced. I don't know exactly how many were made, but I do receive royalty payments.

It was absolutely amazing to have a Big Lo Super Fan action figure made after me! You can see what it looks like on the Internet; I'm wearing my #23 jersey, and I'm holding a big "Number 1" hand sign. There's a big white D and a white picket fence with little stems you can stick into my fists, and two other optional signs, too, so I think it's both fun and funny! They are still being sold online, all these years later. I think it's pretty amazing! I'm the only Super Fan I know who has his own action figure. I think it would be great if there were more action figures for other Super Fans, too. Can you imagine what it would be like to have a collection of 30 or 40 Super Fan action figures?

I did a couple of product signings, and altogether I signed a few hundred of them. One day I was at a Mariners game and I felt somebody tap me on the shoulder. It was a very polite Japanese man, and he said, "Mr. Lo, will you please sign this action figure for me?", and he handed me the action figure in its packaging. "Of course," I said. "I'd be happy to do that." "Yes," he said, "but will you also do that for all of us?" I turned around and there was a line of 27 people! Oh, my gosh! This was during a game, and I didn't want to miss what was happening on the field, but it was quite an honor and I was very pleased to do it.

The group was Japanese tourists who had come to see Ichiro play, and they had all purchased my action figure, so it was really exciting for them and for me. We were on the concourse and I signed all the packages. I took pictures with them, and even though we had a language barrier, it was great to know they appreciated me so much.

My guess is they knew about me because I was once in a Yokohama tire commercial with Ichiro, one that I never even saw! It was something that I got called to do at the last minute. I never got to see the finished product so I have no idea how it came out, but I guess it came out okay. I was on the set with a whole bunch of other people, and we stood around all day. Everybody was looking at each other thinking, "What are we doing here?" They had Ichiro do a few things, but the rest of us were just sort of there. Ichiro and I were star/fan buddies. Ichiro always called me "Big Poppa".

I have friends who live in Japan, and they told me they've seen billboards of me there! I also have a Japanese issue of Newsweek where they show me holding up my Ichiro sign at a game, so apparently I've made an impact. Imagine waking up and finding out you're a star in Japan!

On a different occasion, ESPN flew me out to New York City and put me up at the 5-star Trump Hotel Central Park so I could be on their morning show called "Cold Pizza". I was on the show with Everson Walls, the NFL defensive back who earned a Super Bowl ring. Everson was the other guest, and the funny thing was that the producers put me up in 5-star hotel, but put Everson up in a 2-star dive! He's the big football player and I'm just the big football fan with an action figure. I thought that was pretty funny; I don't know what Everson thought. Anyway, ESPN asked me all kinds of questions about having my own action figure, because they thought that was pretty unusual. It was an amazing trip and an experience that made me feel humble. In my mind, I'm just a sports fan, but with the reactions I get, I'm hearing people tell me, "No, Big Lo, you're more than a sports fan!"

Going to the airport and seeing the Mariners off, the Seahawks off, the Sounders off, and always being there to welcome all of them home, and all the other extra things I do as a fan are well worth it. The athletes appreciate it, and in turn, I am appreciated. As you know, this means a lot to me.

I Interview for "The Biggest Loser"

It was 2005 and I weighed 420 pounds. I was still a lightweight.

I received a call from a friend who told me he'd heard there were going to be interviews in Seattle for the Biggest Loser TV show, and since he knew my mission was to lose some weight, he thought I should know about it. That's when I got a call from King 5 Television, and the voice on the phone asked if I was going to participate in the interview process.

I said, "Yeah, yeah, I'm going down." It wasn't really in my plans, but I made it my plan and went to The Pike Brewing Company, where the interviews were being held. I waited in line for the better part of three hours, and then finally I was brought into the interview room. I was asked questions about my goals, and I told the interviewers a little of my story, including the news about my new action figure. They were surprised. "Wow! No way, really?" I was asked to stick around for a little while because they were going to put me through the group interview process. I did that, and they seemed to like a bunch of us. They told me they'd be in touch. I was fairly happy with myself and confident I was going to be the next Biggest Loser.

A few days later I received a phone call and they said they really liked my story, there was something unique about me, and my energy was strong and positive, so I was invited to another interview. This time the interviews were at the Hotel Monaco Seattle. When it was my turn, I was taken to a room and videotaped. They asked that I create and submit a video telling them about myself, so I did. It was probably a month later when they contacted me and said they loved my story, everything was good, and they were sending me an itinerary; I was to fly down to Los Angeles.

About two weeks before I was scheduled to leave for LA, I

received a call and was told they had found somebody else and were going in a different direction. Talk about feeling devastated! I think I cried for a week! I was rejected by The Biggest Loser! What did that make ME?

I began to eat myself into submission, and I didn't submit. I started eating and eating and eating. When people get depressed, like I was, we get into such a deep state that nothing else matters. So that's how it was for me; I went to The Dark Side and just ate whatever I wanted, and how ever much I wanted, not taking into account what it was doing to me. Over the next two years I put on a couple of hundred pounds and really didn't think about myself. I just kind of got lost.

In the process of losing myself...I eventually found myself again. I went to the Pacific Science Center one day with my niece and nephews. They had this science-scale for the kids; when you stand on it, it tells your weight on Mars and other planets. The kids asked me to step on it with them, and out of the blue the kids jumped off and I was still standing on it. My nephew, Michael, said, "Wow! Uncle Lorin weighs over 650 pounds!"

I was 658.7 pounds to be exact...on Earth.

I was like, "No way!" I was shocked. I had no idea I weighed so much! All I wanted to do was crawl into a hole and die. I never realized I was that heavy. I knew I was fat, and getting fatter, but I didn't know I was THAT fat. I decided right then I was going to cut out sodas and fast foods and do whatever I could to shed some of these pounds. I made some quick adjustments and I lost about 60 or 70 pounds over the course of the next two months.

This was my wakeup call and the kick in the head I needed that really sparked my thinking. No, I didn't want to be this person. I remembered that at the stadiums, when I was heading up the steps, I was stopping a third of the way, huffing and puffing, and it was getting harder and harder for me. I knew I had put myself in this position.

There are people who lash out at me when I say I've gone from 658 pounds to 365. They say, "Well, you never should have gone up to 658 in the first place!" But you know, if you've never been there, you don't know what it's like. Until you're depressed, sitting in that dark, deep hell hole – which is exactly what it is, you have no idea how bad the pain and suffering is. I used to hide my food. I'd go to McDonalds and order two complete meals to go because I didn't want the clerks to think I was ordering all that food for me. That was the hardest part; I was lying to myself and angry that I let myself go like that. Now that I've accomplished so much, I'm happy with myself again. Yes, I've got more to do...but I can also see how far I've come.

The thing is, everyone has something they're struggling with. A lot of times it's something that can't be seen. With me, it was my weight. It was impossible to hide how big I was; it was impossible to miss me! Other people's struggles are not as visible as mine. Some people are struggling with alcohol, or drugs. Some people have a gambling problem. Other people are in failing marriages, or are worried about their sick elders. Maybe you're the parent of a child who's not doing well in school. Some folks have to work four jobs to barely pay their bills.

Some people are quick to condemn others, and I don't know where that comes from. Maybe it's because their own struggles are so difficult that they only know how to hurt others because they are hurting so much themselves. Something I'm grateful for, and which I'm seeing more and more of all the time, is that people are treating each other with kindness and compassion. I think a lot of it comes from our country's difficult economic times, and the several wars we've been in recently. People have been hurting, and many people have chosen to grow through their pain rather than lash out at someone who's also suffering. I think this bodes well for the United States. We are a great nation and we're only going to get better when we use good character and go out of our way to help each other.

Here we are, almost 10 years later, and what really happened was that TV show made me The Biggest Winner...because that's what I am. I look at the title of that show and think, with no offense to anyone who likes the show, "Wow, why did I ever want to be part of a show that called people losers?" I'm not a loser. I'm a winner. And that's the outcome of this whole thing. I'm so much happier with the way I chose to lose weight. On the show, they try to make you lose weight fast, but I've done it steadily with one pound per week. Yes, sometimes it was more, and sometimes it was less; sometimes I even gained some weight. But here it is almost six years later, after I woke up, and I've lost just about 300 pounds, and kept it off, so my goal of losing one pound per week is pretty darn solid.

ESPN Calling

Back in 2005, one of the kids on my football team, Spike
Anderson, had a brother-in-law who was a videographer for
ESPN, and he was working on a documentary program called
"Timeless". The producer at ESPN heard about me through
Spike's brother-in-law, so a team was sent to hang out with me
for a few days to do an episode on Big Lo.

They followed me around for four days. One night they went
with me to the airport when the Sonics arriving home, and they
got some cool footage from the guys there. My dad and Michael,
my nephew, were there with me after midnight, welcoming
the team home. Then the ESPN crew went with me to a Sonics
game; I was on the Jumbotron telling everyone it's game time!

Then, what I especially liked was that the crew came to watch
me coach one of my football practices. A lot of my kids were
from single parent homes, and broken homes, so this was
special for them because they got to have national TV exposure.
In the clip, you can see my boys working out a bit, and doing a
team cheer. They look really good, and I'm so proud of them!
For a kid, it was really fun to be a part of this. Heck, it was really
fun for me, too!

The ESPN crew also came with me to one of the Seahawk games.
After the game, Jordan Babineaux came up and jumped into
my arms, and then Jimmy Williams came over and gave me his
gloves, so that really helped make this into a cool documentary.

 They also wanted to see my sports memorabilia, so they set up
their equipment in my sister's apartment and spent a few hours
recording me, my sister Marlee, and my niece, Britnee, who said
a lot of nice things about me.

To tell you the truth, it was really weird to have a camera crew with me, recording my every move. One of the more awkward moments was when I had to go to the bathroom before the game and needed to say, "Gosh, guys, can you turn the camera and microphone off?" Other than that, the crew was recording every single thing I did. It worked out well, though. It took the team four days to generate a 12-minute final version. I thought they did a really good job telling my story. Of course, this documentary was filmed long ago, and so much more has happened since then, I think it's time for a follow-up documentary!

You can Google "Timeless, ESPN, and Big Lo", and you can watch the documentary online. I think you'll like it...it shows more about who I really am.

Every once in a while, ESPN will rebroadcast the documentary, so I still get responses from people like "Hey, I saw you in the documentary!" That's always fun to hear because the messages in the documentary are good ones, showing not just some parts of my life, but also how important it is to do good work in your community and help those around you. That's something every one of us must find the time to do. We have to help each other, right? We didn't get to where we are without someone helping us!

Super Bowl XL: My Trip to Detroit

2005 was a magical year for a lot of reasons. I was having a good year coaching the kids, and our Seahawks were doing really, really well. Even though they started with a 2–2 performance, the Seahawks went on to win 11 consecutive games, ending the season with a 13-3 record and taking us into the playoffs.

We enjoyed a bye in the Wild Card games, and then hosted the Redskins for the divisional playoffs. We'd just had our best regular-season ever, but nobody thought the Seahawks could win. Luckily, we had home field advantage. I thought it was really cool that Shawn Springs was coming home to play against Seattle, his old team. Sean had played for the Seahawks for seven years before he was traded to the Redskins. The reporters asked him if there was anything he was looking forward to, and he said he was looking forward to getting back to the fans, and especially Big Lo. For someone of his caliber to come back and say he was looking forward to seeing somebody like myself, well, it was a magical moment. The game turned out to be a real battle, but the Seahawks came out on top with a score of 20-10. This was our team's first playoff win since the 1984 AFC Wild Card game against the Raiders.

The NFC Championship game was against the Carolina Panthers. Once again, the media was against the Seahawks! Everyone was saying there was no way the Seahawks could win! But the fans knew better. People who don't know us just don't realize that when you're playing us on our field, it's tough to come in and also play against the 12th Man because we're 68,000 strong! This was one of those magical games where everything went our way, and the first half ended with a score of 17-7 thanks to excellent playing by Matt Hassellbeck and the rest of our team. In the second half, the score doubled, and we had our first NFC championship with a 34-14 result. We were going to the Super Bowl! The fans in the stadium were elated, and it was amazing to see all the confetti flying around, and the raising of the trophy at the end of the game! The electricity among all the fans was incredible, and everybody was cheering and yelling and beyond ecstatic! The energy was huge! People were in the streets for hours and hours that night celebrating that we were going to the Super Bowl. Everybody was happy, in a good mood, and it was just crazy. It was one of the high points of my life, to be a part of that. We were going to the Big Show!

I then began stressing because I didn't know how I was going to get to Detroit to see the game. I was bartending for Shane at Bleachers Pub, and only working a couple of days a week, so I was trying to figure out what I could sell to make the trip. I didn't have a clue about what I was going to do.

That's when a gentleman named Dwayne Clark came to my rescue. Dwayne is the CEO of Aegis Living, a company that's nationally known for the development, construction and management of senior housing projects. He came up to me at a Sonics game and said, "Hey, I hear you're having trouble finding your way to Detroit for the game. We'd like to help you out." So Dwayne showed how big his heart was and helped me financially so I could afford to buy the tickets and make my way back there.

Previously, my buddy, TJ, said that if I could get tickets to the Super Bowl, he'd drive us out there and pay for a place to stay. Well, guess what, TJ? We're going to Detroit! And you're driving! And paying! This was great because I don't like to fly. I get really bad motion sickness, so I only fly if I have to, and it's not a fun experience. I have to fill up on Dramamine, big time. My boss at Bleachers Pub, Shane Toupol, also helped out and made it possible for me to have a comfortable and enjoyable trip.

A few weeks before the Super Bowl, I was contacted by several celebrity event planners inviting me to Super Bowl parties. I was invited to the P. Diddy party and to the Maxim party, so I was pretty excited about that. We were going to get to Detroit about three days before the game, and it was magical thinking that we were going to experience all these incredible moments.

On the ride out to Detroit, I did a couple of radio interviews with sports program hosts. It was a lot of fun driving under the big sky of Montana doing a radio interview on my cell phone with sports people in Seattle and Detroit. We did some sightseeing on the way and saw Devils Tower in Wyoming and Mount Rushmore in South Dakota.

I hadn't seen Mount Rushmore since I was about eight or nine years old, and seeing it again this time, knowing a lot more about life than I did then, this experience was meaningful. Now that I knew more about our country's history, it made a lot more sense about why this monument was made. If you haven't been there, it's absolutely something to see!

We didn't have time to see the Crazy Horse Memorial even though it was so close by; that's on my next trip. I'd also like to see the buffalo at Custer State Park, and visit the Little Bighorn. We saw a lot of the Badlands, and the beautiful rolling hills. As we were driving along, we went through Wall, South Dakota, and stopped off at Wall Drug. That was a really neat place because there were so many activities to do there. I've always seen the bumper stickers and thought, "What is a Wall Drug?" Dad said we'd stopped there when I was younger, but then it didn't make any sense to me. This time it was fun, and I really liked the giant dinosaur.

We left South Dakota and rolled through Minnesota and dropped down into southern Wisconsin; it wasn't long before we were zipping through Chicago and out to Detroit. On the way there, we had that feeling of electricity and excitement, just like before Christmas when you're expecting your presents. Even though all the sports experts said the odds were against us, I felt sure our Seahawks would win.

We pulled into Detroit; we were staying in a hotel about an hour or so out of downtown. That was kind of cool because when we checked into our hotel, we noticed that our room number was 206, which is the Seattle area code. We took that as a sign that we were going to win! Many other fun things like that were happening to us, so it boosted our confidence.

P. Diddy's party was a pretty interesting experience. Snoop Dogg was there. I had done a couple of security gigs for him and he remembered who I was. He was up on the stage and I was on the side talking to a couple of Seahawks who were at the party when Snoop Dogg called out, "What's up? What's up? Oh, heck YEAH! There's Big Lo, the Super Fan from Seattle!" And all these guys turned around and looked at me, wondering, "How the heck does Snoop Dogg know you?" So that was really cool! Snoop Dogg is one of the biggest guys in rap history, and there we were in the middle of Detroit and he's calling me out in front of all the players! That was really cool...

This party wasn't one of those fancy soirées, and it wasn't a party for dress-to-impress. I was in my jeans and T-shirt! We were all having a good time and there were a lot of big-name people who showed up, but the only ones I wanted to rub elbows with were the Seahawks. Nobody else mattered.

The other party I got invited to was the Maxim party, but TJ and I didn't stay very long because the P. Diddy party was the same night. The Maxim party was more of an eye candy event, so you could come and see all the hot girls dancing around. I love women as much as the next guy, but for me it was about the Seahawks and wanting to see our team win the Super Bowl. For real!

While I was in Detroit I did a lot of media spots. I did Detroit media, New York media, Pittsburg media, and a whole lot of Seattle media. I was kind of put out there for all these different networks and sports programs. I was getting a lot of phone calls from different media agents who were trying to book me for interviews. Most of the questions were, "How do you think your team's going to do against the Pittsburgh Steelers?" Being the optimist that I am, I kept telling them, "We're going to win!" I'm always very positive in interviews, and I always talk about the finer things...and the finer things to me are winning games and supporting my team, win or lose.

The big day came and you can't imagine the excitement of walking into the Super Bowl stadium. Everybody was high on excitement! It was an amazing feeling. What surprised me was that there were so many Steeler fans. It looked like there were 80% Steeler fans to 20% Seahawk fans. And it also seemed like the Terrible Towels were everywhere, but when the Seahawk fans started to bring out their towels, we were told to put them away, you can't do that. It felt like everybody was against the Seahawks.

I bumped into several Seahawk fans when we were walking around. I saw my buddy, Nate, and I also saw the governor, Christine Gregoire. I got a nice little picture with her, and I also ran into Mr. and Mrs. Seahawk, Painted Hawk, Cannonball, and others. When we went back to our seats, though, the section that TJ and I were in was mostly Steeler fans. Mostly everything was Steeler fans.

The pregame show was amazing. Stevie Wonder and India Arie began the show, and The Four Tops also performed. There was an on-field introduction of 30 Super Bowl MVPs, so it was awesome to see all these football greats. We observed a moment of silence for Coretta Scott King and Rosa Parks who had recently passed away, and then we were treated to the national anthem sung by Aretha Franklin and others. Tom Brady, the MVP of two Super Bowls, participated in the coin toss, which the Seahawks won.

The battle began, and it was a tough game. There was a lot of punting, and a lot of fouls against the Seahawks. It just seemed like all the chips were stacked against our team, and it's fun to blame the referees...how do you call a chop block on a quarterback after an interception? Some of those penalties made no sense, and a lot of them were wrong, in my opinion. At the half, the score was Steelers 7 - Seahawks 3.

The halftime show was also amazing, with the Rolling Stones, and all the fans in the stadium were having a great time, even though there was this tension about how the game was going to go.

In the second half, we came out and battled again, but it was a really rough ending because we didn't come out on top. I have to say that the Steeler fans around me were really neat and supportive, and a number of Steelers fans came up to me later and said the Seahawks should have won, and they wished us luck for next year and that kind of stuff. It goes to show that good fans have good character.

The post-game ceremonies were fun to watch, though they were bittersweet. Bart Starr brought the Vince Lombardi Trophy to the podium and gave it to the Steelers owner. The stadium was full of confetti and a very happy Steelers-fan crowd, but it was hard to watch our team lose when there had been so many calls against us. The whole experience was absolutely amazing, but the ride home was pretty painful because every single sports talk radio seemed to focus on whether or not the Seahawks had been shafted, or why they were shafted, or complaining that the referees had been horrible, and everybody seemed to feel bad for the 'Hawks. It seems like we got a bad rap, and the five-day drive home was the longest in my life.

On the way back, we swung through Chicago and went to a couple of stadiums to check them out, so we saw Wrigley Field, the Cubs stadium, and the White Sox stadium; we saw the big Sears Tower, and we stopped off for real Chicago pizza, the deep dish kind. We tried all the Chicago foods, and also had Coney dogs, and I finally had my first White Castle burger. You've got to try White Castle; it's kind of a mandatory thing when you go back that way. There was a lot of really fun stuff we got to do, so we escaped the gloom and misery for a little bit now and then.

All in all, though, it was a lot of fun and very magical, just like you would expect. It was good that the players saw me out there, supporting them as usual. I remember there was this one time when I was with Darrell Jackson and Jordan Babineaux. Darrell was in the hotel lobby trying on some jewelry that was brought to Detroit by Josh Menashe of Menashe & Sons Jewelers here in West Seattle. We saw these earrings that were huge, like four and five carat diamonds. Josh handed me this nice watch and he said, "Here, Big Lo. Try this on." So I put it on, and then asked Josh, "What does this set a guy back, $1,000?" Josh laughed and said, "No, 250." I said, "What, $250?" Josh laughed again. "No, $250,000." "Whoa!" I said, as I carefully slid that watch off my wrist. "You can have this back!" I whispered. Holy smokes, to see $250,000 on your wrist is pretty magical!

But not as magical as going to the Super Bowl.

And not nearly as magical as going back to the Super Bowl eight years later and winning!

God's 12ᵗʰ Man

It was around 2006 and I was working at Bleachers Pub. Raph was one of our bartenders, and she walked up to me one day out of the blue and said, "Hey, me and Joe are getting married and want to know if you would do the ceremony!"

I said, "Holy smokes, I'd be absolutely honored to do that, but I'm not a pastor." Raph explained that I could become an ordained minister online, so I did some searching and found out that the Universal Life Church has ordained over 20 million people. I signed up and received my ordination and minister's card about two weeks later. The funny thing was that Raph and Joe weren't my first wedding because my other friends, Sonya and Tony Rossman, came to me and asked if I'd marry them, too. It turned out that their wedding was prior to Raph and Joe's, so Sonya and Tony became my first married couple.

It was weird being a minister when I first started. I was probably more nervous than the bride! I had never done this before so I didn't know how it was going to sound. I wrote the ceremony and put some quirky stuff in there like, "... for better, for worse, with Seahawk wins and Seahawk losses..." I had several funny antics in the ceremony to make everybody laugh and make the moment cheerful and light because sometimes weddings can be boring and drab. I like to make mine saucy and fun!

The ceremony went really well, so I was relieved. Sonya and Tony chose a sand ceremony and the sand was in Seahawks colors. The whole reception was Seahawks-themed...they even had in ice sculpture in the form of a Seahawks logo! Everything about this first wedding was amazing. It was in an old mansion which was a really great setting for a wedding and it made my first ceremony extra special. People came up afterwards and said, "That was really neat, Lo. You did a great job!" So I felt really good about it all. Here I am 48 weddings later, and every one has been special. I know a lot of really great people, so being able to join them in marriage is a real joy to me. God is the quarterback and He gives me the ball and tells me to run with it!

I've done a few other ceremonies, too. There have been a few funerals, and a few vow renewals. I've also performed some marriages at CenturyLink Field, one was at Safeco Field, and several have been in other unique locations. One of the weirdest weddings was at Manresa Castle in Port Townsend for my friends Kevin and Joanna Nesgoda. It's recognized as a haunted castle. We were there for two nights with the wedding party, exploring Port Townsend during the day and enjoying these incredible dinners in the castle at night. Later, when you're in your room, you can hear unfamiliar noises...every creak in the wall, a surprise footstep in the hall outside your room...

I never actually saw a ghost, but on one of the nights I heard this noise in the hallway. I'm a big guy, but I get as scared as the next person. I was too timid to open my door, but the noise wouldn't stop. It sounded like something was scraping on wood in the hallway. I could feel the hairs rising up on my neck! I had this chill going down my back! I was really freaked out! Well, I figured I was in God's hands so I knew I'd be okay, no matter what. The noise had been going on for about eight minutes...

I thought I'd open my door slightly and take a peek through the crack... All of a sudden all that fear turned into a belly laugh. One of the guys in the wedding party had brought his dog, and it was his dog scratching at his door trying to get in! He had been celebrating a little bit too much that night and passed out. I joined the pooch out in the hallway and knocked on the door until he woke up to take his dog inside. It was funny!

Despite the light-hearted ceremonies I perform, I take my ministry seriously. I mostly do wedding ceremonies, but I also am very devoted to God. My relationship with God is private, but I don't mind letting people know that I am available to do

God's service. I think that once people get to know me, they see that I am really a gentle giant.

I grew up with a bunch of kids and we all went to Glendale Lutheran Church. My family was friends with many of the families in the church and we always had Bible studies. I was brought up to be a man of God. All through my childhood I was involved with different church youth groups. My mom and my older cousin, Sherrie, always talked about the importance of God in our lives, and that made a big impression on me. I always talk to God in the morning, through my day, and at night, and I often pray for people. If someone's got a sick child or they're struggling with something, I keep them in prayer. Some of my friends have marriage problems, or maybe just the daily struggles of life that we all go through; it doesn't matter because I keep them all in my prayers. Throughout my whole life I've relied on God. My relationship with God deepened when I was in my late 20s, and has become stronger every day. I know that God is the source of all life, and the source of my happiness. I don't have to have a relationship with a church to have a relationship with Christ. I rely on my Bible, and I rely on God.

My friend Sean, Walla Walla's biggest sports fan.

Sam Dog and the boys from Rain City Catering.

My good friends Keith and his son KC.
Thanks, PEMCO, for making me a Supercharged Seahawks Fan!

A planter box with my silhouette,
made by Chuck at Chuck's Planter Boxes.

Christina, Christian, Jared,
and me with Shawn Kemp, the six-time NBA All-Star.

A photo from my childhood; can you guess which is me?
(My best friend Scotty is in the middle.)

My good friend Anthony!

The Wild Bunch! Me, Jeff Kathan,
Spike O'Neill, and Shannon Love.

TJ and me in Detroit for Super Bowl XL.

Governor Christine Gregoire and me at Super Bowl XL in Detroit.

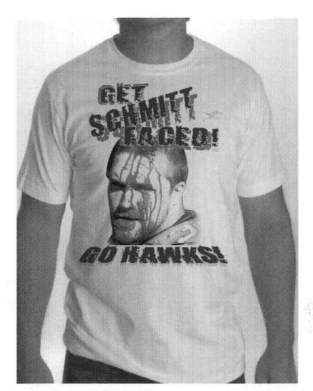

My "Get Schmitt Faced!" shirt idea
to put Jacknut Apparel on the map.

My friend Nick Greer, AKA Chicken Head Red.

Me, Maria Arcega-Dunn and Aaron Levine of Q13,
and Seahawk tackle Walter Jones.

On the set with Chris Egan, Emmy® Award Winner.

Mama Blue, Russell Wilson, and me!

My tribute to Dave Niehaus, "Voice of the Mariners".
Thank you for the memories, Dave.

Friday afternoon before Super Bowl XLVIII, at Microsoft.
I'm on the podium pumping up the Microsoft crowd.

On the Today Show before Super Bowl XLVIII.

The first sign in Seahawk Stadium.

Sending Seahawks off to Super Bowl XLVIII.

Tony Peckham and Dave Krieg visiting me in the hospital.

The shoes LeBron James gave me in Chapter 20, Talent Talent.

Cannonball and Hawkychick.

Me, Samuel L. Jackson, Britnee and Marlee.

Me as the Reaper with Alexi Lalas.

Me and Coach Pete Carroll.

Koren Robinson, Seahawks wide receiver, 2008.

Darrell Jackson, wide receiver, giving me a touchdown football.

Squatch, the SuperSonics mascot,
with the 1978-79 championship trophy.

Jordan "Big Play Babs" Babineaux.

Former Seahawks coach Mike Holmgren.

Me and Robin.

My wrapped 1994 Grand Cherokee Jeep.

My wrapped 2000 Grand Cherokee Jeep.

Me and my action figure!

The Super Fan action figure articulations.

My favorite hydroplane driver, Jimmy Shane.

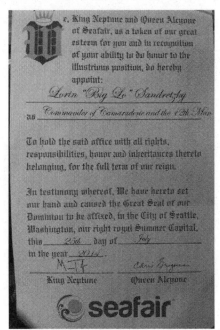

I was knighted by the good folks at Seafair,
and this is the proclamation they gave me.

Mr. and Mrs. Troy Holmes, married 12/12/12 at 12:12 p.m.

Wedding of Kevin and Joanna Nesgoda
at Manresa Castle, Port Townsend.

My Queen Anne team; a not so Little League team, and one of the finest groups of kids I ever coached.

Going over the game plan with my Seattle Interbay Eagles, 2004. We won!

Me and Eric Keith, who wrote the Seahawks
anthem "Better" with VellVett.

Seattle's Mayor, Ed Murray, with me at the Space Needle during the signing of
the 12th Man flag that was headed to Super Bowl XLVIII.

Opening Day, 2006. Delivering the ball to
the podium for Matt Hasselbeck's pitch.

Doing my good deed pulling a neighbor out of the ditch in the winter.

The Super Fan taking it all in...

Let Us Prey

137.6

Just 137.6

'Hawk, yes! We can do better than that!

Everybody reading this book knows exactly what I'm talking about. That's the number we have to beat, and I know we can. And I'm not talking about a measly 137.7 either!

We have to get it up to 140.0, and then we have to get it up to 145.0. This is our responsibility as the 12th Man!

We all know why. When our defensive team is called to play, there have to be 12 Seahawks on the field. You and I have caused false starts, delay of game penalties, made it impossible for the visiting team to hear audibles, and on more than one occasion we've rattled the field goal kicker.

Who's louder than a jackhammer?

Who can drown out live rock 'n roll at a concert?

Who exceeds the sound of a thunderclap?

Who almost matches the sound level of an aircraft carrier deck?

Who creates a magnitude 1 – 2 earthquake?

The 12th Man!

Yeah, Baby! That's us!

We've all heard the details about how the stadium was designed for sound, and how our favorite perch, The Hawks Nest, has aluminum seats to compound our ability to make noise. But all that aside, you can have a well-designed stadium but it's not worth a tail feather without the 68,000 of us pumping up the volume!

Seattle fans have always been known as one of the loudest fan groups in the NFL. In fact, we probably make the other teams jealous with how much love and support and noise we bring to the game. And the thing is, we're standing and screaming for just about the whole three hours. I don't get hoarse after every game like most people do, but it takes me a little while to get my hearing back, but I don't mind! When the game is over, I want to know that I helped our team win.

I think we should have developed a strategy to help us all work together to increase our Guinness record. The best way to start would have been to establish a Committee for the Louder Amplification of Seahawk Supporters, or CLASS. This committee could invite comments from the 12th Man on strategies that could be employed to continually exceed current noise records.

Some of the ideas that have occurred to me, and which I will happily submit for consideration, are ways in which our voices can be used on a tactical and strategic level to unnerve the visiting team. We might also need to consider ways in which we can conserve our vocal strength for key moments when the full force of our combined and deafening clamor can be used to best advantage.

For example, on third down, the east side of our stadium howls as loud as they can when the visiting team is in its huddle, and then is joined by the ear piercing screams of the west side of our stadium when the huddle breaks up and the players lineup for the snap. This 1 – 2 punch might have the effect of completely unnerving the offensive line. Another possibility is our stadium being absolutely silent before a visiting team's field goal kick, but then, just before the snap, all of us together send a sonic bullet directly at the kicker.

I'm sure there are a number of creative ideas among the 68,000 of us that our committee can review, and then recommend the best ideas for field testing. We could then incorporate these ideas into our best practices playbook. Of course, we would need to have a symphonic quarterback to act as our conductor; this person could be made visible to everyone on the giant screens. Heck, in fact, we should probably have our own pregame practice sessions so all our aural assaults are properly coordinated.

Along with high-level strategic planning on the best ways to use our vocal force, I would also like to see a decibel reader installed in some appropriate place, and wired to one of our large stadium reader boards so everyone can see a live reading on our decibel level; I believe our being able to view the magnitude of our vocalization will contribute to our ability, and we will surpass our own clamorous turbulence!

Since our setting the record, the fans in Kansas City have upped the mark, but we all know who won the Super Bowl!

"Won't Power"

I've always had problems with my weight, and everything got
a whole lot worse when I was rejected by the Biggest Loser
television show. As I said earlier, I went into a big depression
and ate whatever was in front of me. I just didn't care anymore.
Two years went by and I was standing on that planetary weight
scale at the Pacific Science Center when my nephew calculated
that I weighed 658 pounds. Make that 658.7 pounds. Anyone
who's tried to lose weight knows how important that .7 pounds
is.

I've tried every diet in the books and on the planet. You name
it, I tried it. I've done Weight Watchers, Jenny Craig, hypnosis,
I've done the 1,000 calorie diet kind of thing, I've tried the 1,500
calorie diet thing, I've tried the 2,000 calorie diet thing, I've
tried the South Beach diet, the Atkins diet, and I've tried every
diet known to humanity. What I found out is that diets die. The
word "die" is in the word diet, so if you go on a diet plan, you can
count on it dying because they all do.

Like I said, I decided I didn't want to be that person, the person
I'd become. I thought about it and I set my goal, which was to
lose one pound per week. I cut out all the deep-fried foods, I
cut out fast foods, sodas, candy bars...I cut out all the obvious
sources of weight gain, which is mostly all the foods you know
are bad for you. I also started working out at the gym in Burien.
The managers there wanted to put me on a different diet, but I
told him, "I'm not going on a diet. I'm just going to change my
ways." They were dubious, but I was resolved. I started eating
more fruits and vegetables, and more proteins; I also ate less
carbohydrates.

I decided that my willpower wasn't very strong, so what I needed
to kick into gear was my "won't power". "I won't eat that,"
and "I won't eat this." I'm at the point now where my Won't

Power works pretty well! All these different lifestyle changes made it possible for me to knock off a pound a week. That's the important point; if you want to lose weight, you have to make a lifestyle change. You can't go on a diet and then revert to your bad habits. You have to lose the weight by establishing a new habit, a new pattern. Otherwise, you just go back to the way you were.

I hadn't eaten fast food in a long, long time, and one day my buddy and I went to McDonald's. I thought, "Well, I don't know if I want to do this..." And it was hard to think about what I'd be putting inside my body after a few years of staying away from that kind of food. I'd read one time about making eating changes, and the article said you have to make choices when you go to a restaurant. You have to learn about mayonnaise and cheese and ketchup and mustard and all the different things that go on a burger. If you can make some good choices, you can avoid all these extra calories.

My buddy said, "Well, just use a little willpower," and I said, "How about I use a little won't power, and I'll get a burger with lettuce and tomatoes and pickles and every vegetable I can find?" So I did, and I ordered a quarter pounder with no cheese, just a touch of ketchup and mustard, and I had the kitchen put lettuce and onions and pickles and tomatoes on it, and it was this big huge mondo-burger that was just delicious! He and I started talking about the whole "won't power" thing, and I liked the way it sounded. I look at all the different ice cream and cakes and pies at times and I think it really isn't will power, it's won't power; if I have will power I will pick it up and eat it. So I decided it's going to be won't power because I won't do it!

My lifestyle changed six years ago and I've lost almost 300 pounds since then, which, if you do the math, comes out to about 50 pounds a year, or about a pound a week. Yes, there were ups and downs. I had a whole bunch of health problems in between and there were times I had to eat certain foods to avoid diabetic problems, or support certain medical conditions I was going through. But by and large, I changed my lifestyle and I changed my life.

There were times when I'd want something sweet, so I asked if I could have a bite of somebody else's dessert, just to satisfy "the want". That was one of the biggest things I learned, which was to satisfy the need or the want for sweets. I didn't have to eat the whole thing! A taste was enough. Do you realize how sweet a candy bar is? Just a slice will do. I learned to enjoy the tiny morsel, instead of cramming the whole bar into my mouth. There's a lot of flavor in a little piece. When you change your thinking, miracles are possible.

I have friends who can eat a whole cake, ice cream, pies and candy bars all day long and they won't gain a pound. For me, I can gain two pounds with a single sniff. It's a bummer when you can't eat certain things but you want to. Well, I learned by taking just a bit of somebody's dessert that "the want" was satisfied, and I didn't want any more for a few days or maybe even a few weeks.

The weight began coming off, and since success breeds success, my new lifestyle became easier and easier to accept. Sometimes there'd be weeks when I was dropping five or six pounds, but then there'd be weeks when I'd gain one or two pounds back. I'd wonder, "What the heck did I do?" I've learned to roll with the punches. I've also learned to take the stairs instead of the elevator, and to park the car at the far side of the lot. I work out several times a week, I eat better and I move more. All these lifestyle changes really worked, and here I am six years later, and I'm down about 300 pounds.

I'm comfortable now where I'm at, but I still want to firm everything up. I'm focusing on doing cardio exercises and moving the parts of my body that have excess skin. My plan has worked so far, so I'm staying positive and I'll keep working on my body. I want to get down to around 330 - 340 pounds, so I'm very close to where I want to be. I owe my success to finding the willpower to say "I won't".

The best thing I could tell people is to think about yourself and what you're putting into your body. If you're consuming 5,000 calories every day and you're not doing the exercise to work off the extra, then you're only making your problems worse. Of course, you have to make sure you're ready for your lifestyle change, ready in your mind, and you have to be ready in your heart. Before you decide to make big changes, if your mind and your heart are not ready, the only won't you'll get is that you won't get anywhere. You must be committed in your mind and in your heart to be healthy. We all know what we should do; but we only do what we're prepared to do. You have the power! Get into your Won't Power!

My Sports Tats

I started getting tattoos years and years ago when I was working in the barbecue restaurant. At the time, I was trying to figure out what I wanted for a tattoo, because I knew I was going to get one and it was time to step up to the plate. I decided I get a tattoo of Joe Camel.

I went to the tattoo shop and spoke with the tattoo artist. He said, "Why are you getting Joe Camel? You don't smoke." I said, "Well, he's cool." He said, "He's not cool. He's got a cigarette in his mouth." "Okay," I said, "don't tattoo the cigarette." "Well," he said, "Even if you only had Joe Camel, it still emulates smoking. I think you should go home and think about it."

After thinking about it for a few days, it happened that we had the TV on at work and then I saw that little Energizer Bunny going across the screen and I thought, "That's me!" I was always full of high-energy, so it seemed like a great first tattoo. To this day, I wonder what the tattoo artist thought about my starting out with Joe Camel and ending up with the Energizer Bunny. I got the bunny on my left arm, and it says, "Energized Hi – Lo Still Going." For years, my theme was rabbits and I added a number of rabbit tattoos.

When I was in the hospital, my buddy, Brian Murphy, visited me and said, "Hey, when you get out of here, let's get you a tattoo!" I said, "Oh, that would be great!" When I was discharged, we went to the tattoo parlor; I thought it was time to get my first tattoo as a fan. That's when I had the Super Fan logo from my action figure tattooed on the back of my neck, along with its barcode! I wanted a scan-able barcode, but it doesn't scan. The next tattoo I got was the Sea-Fence™, also on the back of my neck. This was the start of my sports-themed tattoos.

I really like the artistic work of Cody Hart at Derm F/X, and he said he wanted to do some more pieces on me. That sounded great, so the next one was the Seahawks logo with Jordan Babineaux popping out of it. The next one was Matt Hassellbeck, and then I had Cody add Leonard Weaver. When the tattoos were done I went to the guys and showed them, and they said, "Oh, that's really cool, Big Lo!" I asked them if they would sign the tattoos, which they did, and then I went back to Cody and had him ink the autographs. It was pretty cool!

Soon after, I decided I wanted a player portrait tattoo, so I got Roy Lewis on my left arm. That one took a long time...like three 6-hour sessions and a fourth session of four hours. This one was done by Scotty Tague, so now I had two artists who wanted to work on me, and I had to think up all these neat little ideas. Here we are six years later and I'm about 40 tattoos into it.

Almost all my tattoos are sports-related except for the Energizer Bunny, Thumper, my Trix rabbit, my Nestlé Quik rabbit, and my Sweet 'N Lo tattoos. Oh, and my cats! I've got Oliver on one thigh and Bosco on the other. They're my boys.

My sports tattoos include a women's basketball team, the football tattoos, and the women's lingerie football league; now they're called the Legends Football League. They never wore lingerie, so I don't know why they were called the lingerie football league. Well, I mean I know why, but... They wore boy's shorts and jogging bras and they played as hard as the boys did, I'll tell you that! I've also got baseball tattoos, basketball tattoos, and soccer tattoos. I'd have a lot more basketball tattoos if we had a team, but we do have a wonderful women's team, the Storm; so I also have that tattoo. And, of course, I have a Husky and a Cougar tattoo!

I've got three of the coolest tattoo artists anybody could ever have, so if anyone wants me to get a tattoo about a team or a player, just hit me up. Cody Hart, Scotty Tague, and Chentelle Hitchcock do choice work. Chentelle did my Seahawks knuckles, Clint Dempsey on my neck, and she also did Oliver and Bosco.

All three of these artists are big talents.

I've got plans to get more tattoos, absolutely! I want to put the Super Bowl trophy and the Super Bowl ring on me somewhere. I'd also like to have a Russell Wilson tattoo on me, too. We'll have to wait and see where it goes...

The Legion of Loud

I'm proud of our fans because of the support and love we give our team. We are an exceptional group of fans, unlike any other group of fans in the NFL. We have unified ourselves under the flag of The 12th Man, and we are proud and strong!

We also have a unique group of Super Fans who, in their special ways, "go above and beyond" with their gifts of loyalty and enthusiasm. I've invited four of my friends to express their feelings about their commitment and devotion, and how they view their responsibilities to our team and to all our fans.

Please allow me to introduce Mama Blue, Cannonball, Eric Keith, and Mr. Love!

Mama Blue

I've been a Super Fan since 1976. I've been doing this for 38 years. It's pretty awesome, actually! When I started out, I was just a fan, and my husband and I enjoyed going to the games. I bought season tickets for the Seahawks when they first came into the NFL, as a gift to my husband for his birthday. I was a cheerleader in high school, and he was a football player, so how corny is that? We love football, and we always rooted for the Huskies. Then we rooted for both the Huskies and the Seahawks!

In 1983 I started wearing a blue sweatsuit, and that was when the Sea Gals nicknamed me Mama Blue. I just took it from there, and being a hairdresser, I made up my own wig! I make my own accessories, my earrings, my shoes, my gloves, and it just kind of snowballed! Every year I'd add a little bit more. When we were in the Kingdome, I called it war paint that I put on. Now I get, "See what you started?" Everybody else has climbed on the bandwagon, which is fine! I love the fans!

I got inducted into the Pro Football Hall of Fame in 1999, which was a great honor. One fan from every NFL team was inducted, and I was selected for the Seahawks. I got to raise the 12th Man flag in 2007, which is a great honor. It was the last game my husband, Tricky, was able to attend; he passed in 2007. But anyway, it's just kind of fun to be a fan that everyone knows, especially now, when I'm going to be 84. Like they say, being a fan is not a hard thing to do. You just support the team. I was the booster president of the Seahawkers for 10 years and met a lot of the players in the Chuck Knox days. I'm just doing what seems like a lot of fun! I'm still a hairdresser and work two days a week, so, I just keep on keeping on.

The athletes are awesome, too. They love us, especially the older ones. I love it when they see me and say, "Oh my gosh, are you still here?"

They're all very receptive, and I think they all consider me their mother, or grandmother, or great grandmother. They are a great bunch of people; the whole organization is pretty awesome.

Oh, by the way, I am now a Lego at Bartell Drugs. They made a mini Lego of Mama Blue. I've done one signing, and I'm going to do a couple more. I really couldn't believe it. They decided they were going to do a 12th Woman, so I got a call from a merchandising manager, and he said to me, "You know, I can't think of anybody better to put it out there for than you", so they got my glasses, and they got my boas. They couldn't do my wig, so I'm wearing a hat and a helmet, and I've got a water bottle and a football, but that's okay! The fact that I'm out there just surprises the heck out of me. I have Big Lo's action figure in my collection, of course, and now there's this Lego of me!

You tell Big Lo I'm proud of him and his dedication as a Seattle Super Fan.

One more thing...I would like to thank my three kids, four grands and seven greats for their love and support of Mama Blue; we all bleed "blue and green"! Go 'Hawks!

Cannonball

I've always been a Seahawks fan, and there are many of us who get a lot of pleasure from being a little bit over the top; we enjoy getting into costuming and face-painting because it's fun. Life is meant to be lived with passion and excitement, and I enjoy dressing up as Cannonball and cheering for our team with all the other tens of thousands of Seahawks fans. At the end of the day, we're all united with blue blood under the common flag of the 12th Man!

There are millions of Seahawks fans, and we have a lot of camaraderie for each other because we've all shared the sorrows and the joys over nearly four decades since our team first became an NFL franchise. We've followed this team our entire lives, and it's not really so much about being a fan as it is about recognizing our passion for our team as a way of life. If you visited my home, you would see it's a Seahawks home...our fandemonium shines through because it's the way my wife and I live our lives. We love it! This is who we are. If you cut me open, I bleed Seahawks blue.

Most people have a passion for activities that excite them and bring satisfaction and happiness. I love being Cannonball, and I love being a 12th Man. I also love being in the stadium as the crowd goes crazy with excitement! The bleachers start to shake and you can feel the intense power of the 12th Man. Everyone genuinely believes that when our team is on defense and the opponents make a play, the 12th Man can affect the outcome of what's going to happen on the field. All our voices are united because we believe in the talent and prowess of the Seahawks, and we know we can give our team an advantage by getting

LOUD!

I firmly believe the ball thrown to Crabtree in the final moments of the NFC Championship Game was a little bit short because Kaepernick was distracted by the noise and the force of our 68,000 frenzied 12s! Our roaring sound affected his coordination and upset that last-minute pass.

Think about it! We registered the world record at 137.6 decibels... Do you know how loud that is? Live rock music is a paltry 114 decibels, which is the pain threshold for the average human being. A thunderclap is a meager 120 decibels. A military jet taking off from an aircraft carrier is a measly 130 decibels! The 12th Man makes almost as much noise as an entire aircraft carrier deck, and we sustain the volume! Do you think the 12th Man can interfere with a visiting team's offense? You bet we can!

You haven't lived well until you get home from a game and your ears are still ringing. Then there's the adrenaline...it takes a while just to calm down. We go to a game and win or lose, we still have to unwind from all the emotions and excitement we feel coursing through our veins. One thing about the 12th Man hangover is that people can't understand what you're saying. You're talking in a low whisper because you have no voice...you left it on the field!

We finally brought home the Lombardi Trophy from Jersey this past February. Winning seasons are rare. What we have right now is very special, and we have to savor this moment. We also have to cheer for our team and the day when we get back and do it again. I savor every moment of the game, and every moment of the season.

I was fortunate enough to go to Super Bowl XL in Detroit. One of the coolest things that happened that day was walking toward our seats, and looking down, in the same location in Ford Field as if we were at CenturyLink, there's my bro' Lo sitting there! I went down to his seats and gave him a big old hug! We were there together, and that was special.

My wife, Laura, is Hawkychick. She and I were great friends for 12 years. (Yes, 12!) Then we started dating, and my friend became my girlfriend, my girlfriend became my fiancée, and my fiancée became my wife. Laura is still every bit of all those things to me to this day.

Every time I come to a game I always love spending some time with Big Lo. The 12th Man and the Seahawks define us. I like Big Lo not only because of who he is and what he means to Seattle, but also because he's a true friend. He and I have had many years to build and strengthen our bond, and I consider Big Lo a great friend, and always will.

Eric Keith

You might know me as the rapper who created the Seahawk anthem called "Better". Me and my bro' VellVett made a video of it. We hit it together, and it's on YouTube with around 200,000 views so far.

I've always been a Seahawks fan, and last year catapulted me to a whole new level when everything exploded for me in a really big way. I've always wanted to contribute something that would have a big effect on the fans and the team, but I never had the opportunity until last year. I was blessed to get into the VIP section at training camp, so I was able to see all the players up close and take pictures with them.

Seeing the team working out inspired me and I was thinking, "I gotta do it...I gotta do it!" so I wrote the anthem, and the words and music just poured out of me. It took a couple of months to make a professional recording and also shoot the video. We recorded the video in Hawk Alley before our mid-November home game when we crushed the Vikings, 41 – 20.

Then something else happened that brought everything I do into the light. It was the Friday before the Texans game in late September. I saw a lot of these photos for that week's Blue Friday and there were some weak pictures of Richard Sherman, so I thought, "Let me make something really quick." I'm a graphic designer, so I did my thing. It was in the morning, right before I took the kids to school. I posted it, then dropped off the kids. The next thing I knew, the picture went viral. It was all over Facebook, all over Instagram, people were changing their profile pictures for my art, and I was like, "Oh, my God!" People were just going bananas...it was like I touched lightning!

A friend of mine texted me and said, "Hey, man, your pictures are featured on the Richard Sherman Facebook page!" So I messaged, "Thank you for posting my art," and lo and behold, I got a Facebook Messenger reply!

The dude wrote, "Hey, man, I'm working on some new stuff. Do you want to be involved?" I asked, "Is this Richard?" "No," came the response, "It's his marketing team. I'm Joe Tafoya..." I was stunned! I'm messaging with Joe Tafoya! It was crazy! And this was the start of it...I worked with Joe on some projects, and now I'm being recognized for my art. Soon after, in early December, we dropped the video. On the first day it got 20,000 views, and now we're up to about 200,000 views!

I can't even tailgate now because every time I go down there, we're performing, or somebody wants us to perform. Tailgating has taken on a whole new level for me. When I go to Hawk Alley, it's crazy, and really fun. Everybody is glad to see me and VellVett, and we're getting all these props. I remember this one time I was minding my own business in Rite Aid, just walking up to the counter, and this dude ran up to me and said, "Hey, you're the guy who did the Seahawks anthem!" I'm like, "Yeah, that's me." "Dude! That was so awesome!" he said. It's really cool knowing first hand that I've been a source of happiness for people.

(You can see my work at https://m.facebook.com/erickeithdesigns and http://1onemusic.com/)

Another time I was with my wife, Megan "LaTonya", and we were invited to an award ceremony. It was a red carpet event, and we got to walk the red carpet and get interviewed about my art. We were in the VIP section talking with Dave Craig, Bishop Sankey, Jerry Brewer, and Mike Gastineau...it was so surreal, you know? Megan tweeted, "I can't take nine steps without somebody knowing my husband and wanting to take a picture with him!" I was getting all this attention, and everybody wanted to take a picture of me. I was like, "Man, this is really awesome!"

As awesome as it's been, I recognize I'm new at this, and I'm grateful to all the fans that love the work God brought through me. A shout-out also goes to the Super Fans who are my mentors, so to Mama Blue, Big Lo, Mr. Love, Cannonball, Mr. and Mrs. Seahawk...you're all my heroes! And yo, Big Lo...I know you've got my back. Thank you for being a real friend.

This new experience is really cool because when I was younger, I was never recognized for anything. I mean, I've always been an artist and a musician, and now my talents in these areas are respected. When the anthem came out, and I actually had something to give to somebody, something they actually liked, and loved, it made me feel really good.

The anthem is what I gave, and that's what I'm receiving now, all that joy and love because of the gift that came through me to the people. To be honest with you, I didn't do it for any fame or money; I didn't expect anything at all. I just did it. I did it because of how much of a Seahawks fan I am. I have a talent, and the thing I do is rapping, and I wanted to do it, and I felt like I had a really good song, a song people can listen to before the game and get pumped up, and that's why I did it. The whole focus was to put something good out and show you how much of a fan I am, how much I love my team. And that's what it's about, being a Super Fan.

Mr. Love

My interest in football began by going to games when I was 18 years young, sitting in the front row in 1976 with all my family. At that time, I wasn't a rabid football fan, although, when I was much younger and watching games on our black and white TV, a football player with white shoes caught my eye. I was intrigued and asked, "Who is that?" and Pop answered, "That's Joe Namath." I was sold; he became my favorite player and the Jets were my favorite team.

My father put together a group section in the Kingdome for our whole family and as he explained, it was important for family to share a common love. That's how I got involved, with brothers and sisters and cousins and uncles, nieces and nephews, and friends of friends. We had a great deal of people attending, sometimes as many as 50 season seats. My mother, Pamela Love, the artist, and our family used to paint these giant posters. They were nine feet tall and 30 feet long with inspirational statements and life-size silhouettes of players. We were constantly uplifting the team and the fans, sending that message out as a family, and cheering. We bonded as a family and as a group, and then we bonded as a franchise and a fan base.

I had to learn how to be an NFL fan. A lot of lessons were learned in these new and developing years, and love and affection was created for the sport, the game, the bright colors, the soon-to-be lifestyle, but more importantly, I found myself fascinated with the crowd. Everyone else would talk about the Seahawks' stats, the players, the game details, and all of that was interesting, but it never captured me. What captured me was the energy in the crowds, the connection, how chants could be started, and how the energy would flow among the people, and how the energy was really high some days and really low on other days. I took it on myself to really learn from what I was feeling. I become a participant, and then a leader, and eventually an ambassador.

Most people remember Bill the Beer Man. He handled his
activities on the north-end of the Kingdome and would make
appearances around the stadium; I was anchored in the south-
end and took great pride in defending our South End. Never
did I let the North End out-cheer the South End! Back in the
beginning, when the Seahawks weren't a household name,
weren't really feared or respected among NFL circles, we were
just a new franchise. As fans, we didn't have a unified structure.
When we first started, we were Packer fans, Charger fans,
Steeler fans...there really weren't any Seahawk fans, and we
were a melting pot of NFL franchises. The unification was all
to come. There was a lot of confusion on how to act, and how
to cheer. A culture hadn't yet been established. Eventually, we
brought the Wave from Husky Stadium and made it our own,
and made it pretty famous. This is how our identity began to be
built. When Bill the Beer Man left to work other stadiums, my
family and I anchored that South End and kept the Waves and
cheers and defensive calls coming, and it was quite exhilarating.

I would stand up in the front row in the Kingdome and address
the extremely quiet crowd at times, and then I'd let out my
cheer, from the diaphragm. I was once an opera singer, so I was
able to project those notes of inspiration, and challenge our
fans! One of the things I used to always say was, "Do not boo,
and do not blame the Seahawks for losing. Did we do all that we
could do? Did we cheer? Were we loud?" I challenged the fans
back then by saying, "We have a job to do!" I would sing out,
"We are the Seahawk fan base, we are the 12th Man!" I would
run up and down the aisles, talk to people, and get the energy
to grow and blossom and commit. This was good 12th Man
leadership!

I believe anybody can be a Super Fan. I encourage that, and I
encourage people to dress up. When we got our new Seahawk
Stadium, which is what it was first called, I started dressing
up in colorful suits, hats, ties, nice shoes...dressing kind of
"brightly". I want people to express themselves in colorful and

expressive ways. People see how I dress and how I act, and it encourages them to follow suit (pun intended). Encouraging people in this manner has helped build our identity and the brotherhood of being a 12th Man.

I'm most proud of being part of the movement, of being part of the brotherhood and sisterhood where everybody's a star, everybody has an opportunity to be whatever they want to be. This is what I most cherish...continuing the belief and brotherhood of the 12s.I feel like I am an ambassador, a man of peace, goodwill and good sportsmanship, and that I help by carrying on the teachings and the traditions of what it means to be a 12th Man; if I could be remembered for anything, it would be for this, passing on the tradition.

Big Lo and I both embrace the idea of good sportsmanship and being a positive fan, of being present for your team and setting a good example. I was taught by my father, Judge Love, that in all situations you had to be above reproach, and I've always demonstrated this as a representative of the fan base. If you see bad sportsmanship, you have to go to that person with the courage to speak up. Some fans really don't know. They may only be a fan of one or two years and haven't been taught the best way to be a good fan. I'm not the fan I was in Year 1, or Year 5, or Year 12. I've evolved dramatically over the years.

I've done some bonehead things! I've yelled at refs once in awhile, and one time, at a player who was injured on the field. I turned around and saw all the quiet fans behind me in shock as I berated a hurt player...and that look in my father's eyes. Then I realized, "Oh, my God, I never should've said that!" Now I see other fans doing these same things and I can see they don't know. It's their learning curve, and when they tell me how upset they are because our team lost and they want to blow up, I tell them this is part of learning how to be a fan, learning how to deal with loss. You also have to learn as much about dealing with victory as you do about losses. I think we're pretty respectful, we don't gloat too much, and we pay homage to other teams. All those years of losing has made our franchise a great winning franchise.

There's not a better feeling in the world than when I travel around the country. I go to a lot of away games, and I'm recognized by a great deal of people. They appreciate my being there, they appreciate what I stand for, and when I go to those away games, I conduct myself very respectfully, and I act as the crowd around me acts. The expected behavior is different in every stadium, and you have to adapt to the people around you and follow their lead when you are at an away game. You have to show respect, and you can't act like you do when you're in your home stadium. At home, we have different traditions to follow.

The higher up you go in the ranks of being a Super Fan, the more people are going to be jealous, and angry, and tear you down, and as many people who love you, there are as many who hate you. There are also a lot of people who don't know you or know anything about you, so it's about managing the love, and managing the hate. It takes a toll on a person. You have to be careful not to react negatively or overzealously. You can't take all the love in and let it go to your head, either. It's not easy, and there are some challenges with this. I've decided I'm just going to be me, and do what I feel is right in a balanced and thoughtful way. I'm going to try to set an example by doing what I do.

Right now, the most important aspect of my life is being a 12. I'm a fan who cares. Being a 12 empowers my life in a positive and healthy way, and it's an honor. I'm going to continue spreading the love and perpetuating the values of what a 12 is, with all the passion, the excitement, and the dedication of being a 12th Man.

Talon Talent

One of the coolest Seahawks I've ever met is Jordan Babineaux! Jordan played cornerback, safety, and was on our special teams. After every single game he'd come running into the end zone and jump up into my arms! He did that after every home game for over a year, and it was so much fun to have a player who cared about the fans that much. Everybody around me loved it when he came and did that! It was kind of a tradition. We haven't found anybody yet who took his place, though Roy Lewis did a good job for quite a while, too!

With Jordan, I can just call him up on the phone, and if I'm having a bad day, he'll turn my frown upside down. He's a very kind and caring man! One day I'm expecting to enjoy some of his special gumbo, because I've always heard about the gumbo but never got to try any, so Babineaux, if you're reading this right now, I want some gumbo!

Roy Lewis was another great Seahawk. He started out playing for the Huskies, and then was signed by the Pittsburgh Steelers as an undrafted free agent. Later he joined us as a Seahawk, and when Jordan left to play for the Titans, Roy Lewis took me under his wing and made sure that if I ever needed anything, like a ticket or an invitation to an event, he'd get it for me. "Is everything handled?" he'd ask, and I always said, "Yes, sir!" My first-ever portrait tattoo was of Roy Lewis, and that was really cool because when I got that done, Roy was pretty excited. I've never seen anyone so excited about somebody else's tattoo. Roy was overwhelmed by it and he was always pulling me around by my arm so he could show "his" tattoo to everybody. That was kind of fun and it touched my heart.

Most people don't know that some of the athletes are quite friendly and open. Because they're so well known, people assume they're uptight and stuffy, when actually a lot of these athletes, not just our Seahawks, but our Mariners and Sounders, too, are very approachable. People usually ask me, "Say, Big Lo, how do I get an autograph?" and I always tell them, "You have to hang and wait for them to come out of the locker room!

Sometimes they'll be in a hurry, and sometimes they've got all the time in the world. But if you're there, and you've got a big smile on your face, your odds are improved!"

Matt Hasselbeck was another great leader for the Seahawks, and he's a guy who, whenever he saw me, he shook my hand and gave me a hug. He was always straightforward, and friendly, and you could tell he loved the fans. He was a great leader on the field, and a great leader off the field. Whenever he threw events, like a golf or bowling event, he was genuine every time. He was easy to approach, and that's nice to see in a professional player, because part of being a celebrity athlete is signing autographs and taking pictures with people. It's not that hard to do and doesn't take much time, but sometimes some of the guys get in a big hurry and are tied up in their own lives and in their own thoughts. I understand that; but it's really great when an athlete will give some time to the people who admire and respect their athleticism.

Matt Hasselbeck was always jovial, and kind, and he's a genuine and wonderful person. I've got the last shoes Matt wore as a Seahawk, and that's quite an honor when you think about it. Matt was pulling out of the Seahawks practice facility, and my buddy David and I were there. David's one of those guys that likes to go to the VMAC and wait for the players to finish practice. He just kind of hangs out and waits for the players to leave, and then he asks for autographs.

It was the day after our season ended in a playoff game against the Chicago Bears. Matt came driving up and he said, "Here you go, Big Lo! The last shoes I'll ever wear as a Seahawk!" and I said, "I hope not!" but that's the way it was. I was really bummed because he said it was his last game as a Seahawk. I hate to see the players go because that's one of the things that make the team what it is. It's the players, and when your favorite players move on, it's hard to say goodbye. I'm kind of sentimental that way because I like people, and my favorite athletes are important to me. Another player who also needs to be mentioned among my favorites is Darrell Jackson; he was always very good to me. Thanks to him, I have three touchdown footballs he gave me right after scoring. I think it's time we start a campaign for Darrell Jackson to raise the 12th Man flag! There are always new athletes to admire and enjoy, but that doesn't make it any easier to let my old friends go.

Another standout is Kobe Bryant, one of my favorite players of all time in any sport! We met during his rookie season. I was standing by the locker room with some other fans, and a little kid was standing there beside me. Kobe came walking out and the kid says, "Hey, Kobe, you're going to be the next Michael Jordan!" I looked at the kid and then I looked at Kobe and said, "No, he's not, he's going to be The Kobe Bryant!" We hit it off immediately and started chatting. He asked me for my address and about two weeks later, a box arrived with a pair of game-worn shoes from Kobe Bryant. Kobe is one of those guys I'll always think of as a gem. He's a guy that cares about his fans, and that's really cool. After Kobe 's last game here in Seattle, at the Key Arena, he came walking out of the locker room with a pair of shoes and they went right to me. It was really incredible! He's always been a great guy, throughout all the years of knowing him. I have several of his game worn- jerseys and probably about five pairs of his shoes.

Then there's LeBron James. This LeBron James anecdote is a long one but it's a good one! In his first year playing against the Sonics, LeBron was down by the locker room area and his agents, Eric and Aaron Goodwin, introduced me to him and said, "This is Big Lo. Big Lo is a really big fan, he's a great, loyal fan..." So I shook LeBron's hand and said, "It's really nice to meet you, LeBron. I love your game, I love what you do, you're fun to watch and I just want to say thank you." He said, "Hey, thanks, no problem." Then I said, "LeBron, would you mind signing my ticket stub?" He said, "No, I only sign for little kids and good-looking women." So I said, "Can I get a picture of you real quick?" and he said, "No, I don't do pictures, man." "Wow," I thought, "This is a bummer!"

The next year rolls around and LeBron comes back. This time I have my two nephews, Michael and Steffen, with me and I said, "Hey, LeBron, would you mind signing for my nephews?" and LeBron said, "No." So I asked, "No you won't sign, or no you don't mind?" He replied, "Not right now," and he walked away. I thought, "Wow!" Now it's the third year and LeBron comes walking out. Craig Ehlo, one of our former SuperSonics players, was there with a bunch of Boys and Girls Club kids. So I called out, "Hey, LeBron, would you mind signing for the Boys and Girls Club?" and he's like, "Oh, I'm busy, I have to go," and away he went...so I'm just standing there like, "Are you kidding me?"

Now the fourth year rolls around and again LeBron's walking by. This time there's this pretty lady with a LeBron James jersey... and he refuses her, too! He walked right past her without a word and didn't sign her jersey! Holy smokes! I couldn't believe it! But then he saw me, and he came back and shook my hand, and I was amazed! What? Is this for real? LeBron actually shook my hand! Did Hell just freeze over? What's going on here? I better go play the lottery! It was really funny because here he was, all of a sudden being nice to me. LeBron got on the team bus, waved to everybody, and off they went!

The last year the Sonics played, LeBron came walking out of the locker room and I saw he had a pair of shoes in his hands... and I was thinking, "Oh, God! What I would give to have those!" And he was walking, walking, walking...and he comes walking right up to me! I thought, "Oh, he's just going to mess with me..." He handed me the shoes and he said, "Here you go, Big Fella! This is for all the years of crap you put up with!" I almost passed out! I almost fell over backwards! I almost died! He's one of the best players in the NBA, and he hands me his shoes! Holy smokes! I was in hog-heaven and complete disbelief! As he walked away, I called after him. "Hey, LeBron!" and he turned and he said, "Yeah? What's up, Big Fella?" I said, "You're still a jerk!" It made him laugh and I got the last word in, so it felt good. I'd like the opportunity to see him again and say thank you, and let him know I think he's still a jerk.

I've got a good baseball story, too. I'm not just about one sport, you know. I want people to realize I'm a multisports fan. There are people who like just football, and people who like just baseball, and people who like just soccer, and people who like just basketball, but there's nobody else like me who goes to all the games. I love sports of all kinds, and I'm a Super Fan of all our teams.

I remember the time...it was 1997, and I was in the seats behind the Mariner's dugout, standing by the front row there, and a bunch of players were below, huddled in the dugout. All of a sudden this hat comes flying up and I grab it and this guy pokes out and looks at me and says, "I just wanted to make sure you got that!" It was Ken Griffey, Jr. and he had tossed up his hat from the All Star game! Griffey is one of those guys I always wondered about because so many people talk poorly about him... "Oh, he doesn't sign autographs...he yelled at my kid...he wasn't very nice to me..." and people say so many different things about him that are bad. But he was very nice to me, and I appreciate it.

Here's another good football story. I began smacking my Sea-Fence™ sign and making noise with it during the same time when Al Harris was playing for the Philadelphia Eagles. All the commotion and noise drew a lot of attention from the players because when they're down near our end zone and they hear that sign smack, they're always looking to see who the heck's making all that noise? After a game one time, Al Harris came running up to me and he handed me his gloves and said, "I just want to let you know you're the best fan in the NFL, man. I've never seen anyone who cheers like you!"

It feels really good when you hear a player say something like that! Not only do you realize that this star athlete is recognizing your effort, but also that the other players are hearing and recognizing your support. Since then I've had about seven or eight players from different teams come up to me and say, "You know, you go harder than we do!"

Most people just yell at the games...they scream and they holler. Me, I yell and holler and I'm smacking that sign a lot, so I get a workout! I usually leave a Seahawks game spent, absolutely exhausted. I'm there for five or six hours depending on when I get through the gates and how long the game takes, so it's work! But it's like going to the best job on the planet!

'Hawk Pride

Though this chapter is about 'Hawk Pride, you have to remember that I am a multisport fan. In our area we're fortunate to have more than one great team. I've got 'Hawk Pride, Mariners Pride, Sounders Pride, Storm Pride, Husky Pride, Cougar Pride, Mist Pride, and anybody else I've missed! I go to high school games, middle-level and elementary games...they all have meaning for me! I have a deep love for sports of all kinds, and I'm proud of my team whether they win or lose. That's just the way it is.

These are my guys, these are my gals. They're out there representing me, our city, our region, our state. Because they're representing us and all the great things about where we live and what we're about, I have a deep pride for them. It's not a case of having to win all the time to impress me, or to make me proud of them. The only way I could be more proud of our teams is if I was on the teams, too! That's not going to happen, so the next best thing I can do is let them know how much I care.

Lots of fans get caught up with watching the win-loss columns, and I suppose some fans limit their interest to the statistics. But for me, the team is composed of people I care about, and so while I want them to win because winning always feels better than losing, it really doesn't make a lot of difference to me because I care about each and every athlete on that team. They are all important to me. They are all real people, with families, with struggles, with emotions...these people laugh, they cry, and they are putting themselves out there every week, in public, vulnerable to our opinion about their performance. I think that deserves our respect. Think about it. Don't you care about your friend's family, or the family of your neighbors? Well, for me it's the same thing. I happen to be a strong fan, and these people matter to me.

This attitude was instilled in me in high school. My school mates were my brothers and sisters, we were part of the same family, and I was taught that you root for your team no matter what. This is the basis for all strong relationships. You can't have a happy and healthy family life if the mom and dad are arguing all the time, or brothers and sisters don't get along, or if nobody cares about Grandma.

The thing to remember is that we're all in this together, and it's only by being strong in our relationships with each other that we can build a better way of life for each other and ourselves. When you have many healthy families, you have a healthy community. When you have many healthy communities, you have a healthy nation. I think sometimes we forget how important it is to support each other. When times are tough, people usually join together, and that's a good thing. Too often, though, we only do this when times are tough. Think about the magnificent outcomes we could have if we stayed bonded to build a better way of life for ourselves, our children, and all mankind?

When you support your team, you're strengthening your family. I happen to be a Seahawks fan; I'm not a Cowboys or Steelers or 49ers fan, obviously. But I respect those teams and those athletes, too. Those players also have families, have struggled through adversity, have worked hard to be where they are, and their sacrifice also needs to be honored. That's why I don't boo at games. I could never boo, because I appreciate how much work and discipline it took for these men and women to achieve what they have.

There are things we can all do as fans to support our team. Every once in a while I'll build a new sign and take it with me to a game. I put a simple positive message on it like, "I Believe!" or "We Believe!" or a few words the players can see that makes them think, "Okay, there's a guy who's behind us, so there must be more people who are also behind us..." Sometimes just a little effort can make a huge difference for a team. I mean, can you imagine being in front of 68,000 people, being booed? How is that going to help your team do better? I really never understood how some people get into booing and mocking their own team. If you can't say something nice, don't say anything at all, right?

Another thing a fan can do is to get to the game early. If you're there early enough, you'll see a few players and you can call out to them and say, "Hey, man, I really believe in you guys! I love watching you play. Just keep doing what you're doing!" Wouldn't you play better if you had fans that said that to you?

Even if you can't attend the games, you can reach out to your team through social media. Social media is there for a reason... there's Facebook, Twitter, Instagram...you can use this media to send positive vibes like "Go Mariners!" or "Go Seahawks!" When you post something positive, it has a ripple effect. Other people will see your posts, and they might be inspired, too. Sometimes the players check their Facebook or Twitter messages and they'll see these positive posts and that will make them feel good inside, and might make the difference between just performing well or inspiring them to perform at their peak. When the world is beating you up, it's very hard to rise above the negativity; it's an extra task that consumes energy. However, if you're receiving positive messages and compliments that show your fans have faith in you, it's much easier to build from that strong and healthy level.

I used to be big on sending fan mail to players, but now the best way to communicate is through social media. It's amazing how times have changed because now, with the people in your life, we spend more time texting than talking on the phone. Because it's hard to communicate your feelings through a text or through social media, you can also go one step further and head over to the airport, bringing a sign with you. When the buses are leaving, you can wave your sign, such as "Have a Good Road Trip!" to charge up the team, just to make them feel their fans care and are going above and beyond. When you're on a road trip, you want someone to wish you well!

With the Mariners, you can go to Safeco Field by the parking garage; that's the only way the buses can pull in and out, so it's a great place to see the team off or welcome them home. I've gone there for years. There are all kinds of avenues for people to show their support if attending games is difficult. There usually aren't many people joining me to see the Mariners come and go, and I wish there were. With the Seahawks, we now have a group, and we all get together to see them off and see them home again. This is a group of people I've grown to love, and now we're like family. We're all hanging out together, visiting, and cheering as the team rolls by. It's really kind of special!

Sometimes I'll tweet on Twitter, "Hey, Richard Sherman, do me a favor and put your cell phone up to the window so we know you guys see us!" and as the bus rolls by you can see a cell phone up against the window! He's done that a couple of times and it makes us feel good. We know the athletes are reading their Twitter messages and showing their support for us, too!

It's not that hard to find out when the team is leaving or returning. I've been doing this for a long time; all you have to do is figure out how long the flight is, and then do the math. It's really pretty simple. If you really want to do something and take the time, you can find the answers. You can also follow me on Twitter because I'll make an announcement about it. We all gather and wait by the airport. There are also some fans that wait by my buddy Kenny's 76 station just down the road from the airport. When the team comes pulling out, we're standing on the side of the road. This is the love for the team...this is what we fans do...this is what it's about.

People think it's about getting autographs or photographs...but that's not it. It's about showing your loyalty to your team and how much you love them. People call me a stalker because I'm always there, waiting for the plane or the bus...but it's just about showing love. I've been doing this for 17 years. You should come with me. It's a lot of fun, and it makes a big difference.

Fanomenon

For those of us who are already sports fans, this comes as no surprise. Being a fan of a team, any team, is a positive influence on our health, attitude, and social relationships. It helps if our team is having a great season, but even when our team isn't doing so well, there are lots of benefits. I'm not going to roll out all the research...that's easily available to anybody who wants to look for it.

Introducing your children to sports and providing the opportunity to be on a team could start your children on a healthy path, and might lead to their interest in high school, collegiate and professional sports. Being on a team teaches kids to work together for common goals and a whole list of desirable attributes. If you're a parent with kids who are on a team, you know how exciting it is to be on the sidelines cheering for them.

Being a fan of any team makes your step a little more lively, and you can feel the goodwill, bonding and connections with many of the other parents. If you raise your kids to be sports fans, you're setting up a pattern for good family bonding, and all the lessons that come with watching professional athletes (perseverance, courage, leadership, self-control...). When you're a fan, it's a great way to make new friends, and, of course, if your team is doing well, your emotional level is more positive and you feel better about things in general.

Because our team won the Super Bowl, there are now even more positive connections between people. When you put on a Seahawk jersey or cap around here, you're likely to get extra smiles, positive comments, and maybe even a great discussion about our team's merits in the current season.

Sure, we know that sports fans have higher self-esteem and are a lot less lonely than the general population. In fact, in Seattle right now, there's a very strong sense of family and community because so many people identify with our great team. The Seahawks are a focal point for several million people, and that's a pretty big family! The Seahawks have created a sense of belonging that exceeds the awareness of our differences. We're more alike because we have the 'Hawks in common. We identify with each other more easily, we recognize in others the same passion we have, and this commonality, this shared understanding, has brought us together, and holds us together. This is a very good and wonderful thing because it's unified us and helped us bridge to one another. Everybody wants to be connected and loved. The Seahawks have expanded our personal boundaries.

This is a common outcome for all the professional franchises, but for us, here in Seattle, I believe there is something more significant going on. In our case, our fans actually believe they are part of the team. When we call ourselves the 12th Man, we're serious about it. Whenever we field our team, there aren't 11 players on the field, there are 12! And together, at 68,000 fans in the stadium, that's a lot of extra players! That's why we rock the house!

You might think I'm crazy, but a fan's real connection with the team isn't the game, but the amazing emotional experience of feeling the game. There are ups, and downs, and more ups, and more downs...it's seldom a straight ride up or a straight ride down... and when we feel these roller coaster emotions, we feel them together, we feel them as one. Remember being in a comedy club, and everybody laughs at the same time? Or you're at a play and something sad happens onstage, and everybody says, "Ohhhh..." at the same time? What you're seeing is everybody feeling the same thing at the same moment, so it's a shared emotional experience. From what I can see, this group response makes us feel connected to each other.

As Seahawk fans, we are a unique group of people. We're from the Great Northwest, the land of salmon, apples, and Pearl Jam. We have giant mountains with glaciers, thousands of miles of shoreline, and thousands of acres of forest wilderness. We recognize our good fortune to live in this very beautiful country.

Because of who we are, our fan psychology is a little bit different. Something unique has been born here, and I believe we are more passionate about our team than any other fan base in the United States. Come to our stadium early on game day, meet the fans who have gathered, talk to them about their love of the team, witness their enthusiasm before the game begins, watch our stadium explode with excitement as our team takes the field, join us when we rise in our role as the Great 12th Man, wild for our team, crazy with our love and devotion, mad with our joyful passion, inspired by our power, shouting, roaring, howling, and screeching like a savage Seahawk!

Fandemonium

You know how excited you can get when you're watching a game! There is all the drama, and all the hope, and all the anxiety! Games are full of emotion and great stories. A really exciting game can bring you up to the top, slam you down to the bottom, and bring you back up to the top again! That's because your emotions and your passion are tied to what you're experiencing, and that's what I love about sports. When I was a player on a team, I was into all that emotion in a very deep way. Now that I'm a spectator, I'm still deeply into it, but in a whole different way.

That's what I want to talk about in this chapter...taking this tremendous passion and energy you feel as a fan and harnessing it and channeling the enthusiasm and power into contributions that benefit your community. Remember what I was saying before...we are all part of the same family and we all have to find a way to give back. Take a look around at all the wonderful blessings in your life. You have food in the fridge, hot water for showers, a warm dry home...once you start counting your blessings, you'll be amazed at all the people and things that make your life safe and happy. Not everybody has that and I believe all of us need to come together and offer our enthusiasm and kindness to the people who could use a hand up. A real Super Fan is not just a fan of the team, but also a fan of their community.

I think everybody has it in them. We all have the ability to give. Some of us can give a lot, and others have to start out by giving in small ways. This is our house, our community, our nation, and there's a lot that needs to get done. We can't do everything, but when we all do something, a lot gets done. When you see somebody struggling, see what you can do, even if it's only a kind word of encouragement. When someone asks you for a contribution to a good cause, you can shake loose a dollar or two. If everyone gave a dollar, a lot of people would get the help they need. If you hear that somebody is sick, bring over a batch of soup. If someone's in the hospital, like I was, you can take an hour to go by and cheer them up for a few minutes. You don't have to do much to make a big impact. Think about all the ways you've been blessed, and then find a way to spread it around. I'm not saying you have to give everything away, but when we all do a little, everyone in our family benefits. The day will come when you will also seek compassion and kindness, and with a healthy family around you, you'll receive it.

If you want to take a more active role, you can be a leader and do a spaghetti feed to raise money for families that are down on their luck, or families who have a sick child and are not doing well, and they need money for an operation or something. Just open your eyes and see what needs doing, and then try to do whatever you can to help.

Of course, Thanksgiving and Christmas are good occasions for helping others. How nice it would be when we do something all the time. I have a friend who sends a few dollars every month to a local mission to feed the homeless, and another friend who does the same thing for paralyzed veterans.

You can start a food drive, or raise money for school supplies. This year I helped raise money so the principal and teachers could buy backpacks and school supplies for every child who needed them. There are so many different things you can do like that. Just take your passion, your enthusiasm, your energy, and transform it into a positive force that benefits the kids next door or the family down the street or a friend who needs to know you're there and you care. I've heard about kids whose parents have died or something tragic like that, and they're being shipped off to their aunt in Kansas City. When I found out they didn't have anything, I held a fundraiser to buy clothes. The great thing is that everybody can take a moment to pitch in and help out.

A few years ago my buddy, Shane, who owns Bleachers Pub, and his sister and all the girls at work there started helping out the community of Ballard, and they were so successful they were called the Ballard Angels. They would gather presents and dinners for the families that needed some support. I thought that was terrific, and that's when I realized I could also do something similar that was cool and admirable and helped people.

I switched it up a bit, and began making envelopes that had different things in them like prizes and coupons, and I started selling them for $25 each. With the money we raised, we would go out and surprise the different families we'd find. I was coaching at the time so I knew a few families that were down on their luck. I also went to the community centers and schools so I could speak with the counselors, or I'd ask the office ladies if they knew some families who could use a little help. People were really wonderful telling me, "Hey, well, I know this family...", so that's how I got started. Once you get the ball rolling, it keeps growing over the years. This is my 10th year as Santa's Biggest Helper.

I started out helping three or four families, and then it became 10, and then it grew to 25, and last year we helped 33 families. Isn't that awesome? This is what I mean about being a Super Fan. Fandemonium can do extraordinary things when you harness your enthusiasm and direct it toward doing good, toward helping the people in our collective family. Take the excitement and passion you have for sports, and transfer this power into your community. Start small and Go Big!

Live Your Fan-tasy!

I want to talk to you about something super important, because this will make all the difference in your life. We live out here in the Great Northwest and are exposed to a lot of ideas some people think are wacky. They might be wacky, they might not. Most people in our area are open to new ideas, wacky or not! I mean, it wasn't too long ago when the idea of getting acupuncture was considered really wacky, and now it's pretty mainstream around here.

What I want you to do is become a fan, a great fan, of yourself. I'm saying it to you in a way you've not heard before, but it's a message you've heard many times. Maybe if you hear it from me in a new way, it could make a big difference in your life or in the lives of the people you love and care about.

When you're a fan of yourself, it means you do things that help you become better than you are. I know you have a tremendous amount of potential inside you. Some of us know how to tap this potential and use it to create a healthy life, a life of love and fulfillment, a life that's lived at a higher level, whatever that means to you.

All of us are going to be around for maybe another 10, 20, 30 years or more. That's a long time, and we can choose to do something good with the time we have, or we can choose to just live day-to-day, come what may, and let time pass through our fingers.

For me, my choice is to use my time on what I feel is most important. True, sports are a big part of my life, but I also recognize that underneath my love for sports is an underlying source of power and enthusiasm. I want to make a conscious effort to do good in my own life, in the lives of my family and loved ones, and for my community, my country, and my planet.

We all have 24 hours a day and seven days a week, and we're always making choices about using our time.

Since I want to be a great fan of myself, and believe me, it took me a while to figure this out, I want to eat foods that are good for my body, I want to get enough sleep every night, I want to take right action when I'm challenged by a situation, and I want to have a positive attitude so I can be my own best cheerleader and a strong support for everybody I meet.

As near as I can tell, human beings have four key parts to them. There's the body, the mind, the emotions, and the spirit, and each of these need to be cared for properly. When you're a fan of yourself, you make sure you're healthy in every way. As an extension, you also make sure your family is strong and has what they need, too. Going a step further, you go out of your way to help your community. If there is a fundraiser, you make a point of going. If you know a child needs something, you do your best to provide it, even asking others to help out if you can't do it all by yourself. If you know there is a family that's in trouble, you turn toward them instead of turning away.

Aren't you tired of hearing all the bad news? I know I am, and I want to see a big change, a change we can all make when we do this together.

Here's what I recommend:

1. Let's make a commitment to be better than we are now.

2. When we finish reading this chapter, let's put the book down and do something nice for somebody nearby. It could be your wife, your husband, your child, or the neighbor next door, but you're going to do something nice for somebody right away.

3. And you're going to do something nice for somebody every day. There's a lot of merit in doing one good deed per day; I'm challenging you to see if we can do three good deeds a day!

4. One of these good deeds must be telling someone how much you appreciate them, and how glad you are to know them. When we start spreading goodwill around, we're raising the bar and that good energy will ripple and keep making more good vibes. Make it go around so it will come around!

5. Support your team. There's your family's team, your community's team, and our country's team. When you see a way you can help and make a difference, step up.

6. If you have a dream, start making it come to life. This time next year you can be in the same place you are now, or you could be 365 steps further down your road. If you want to learn a foreign language, in 365 days you can know 365 new words or phrases. If you want to learn a craft, in 365 days you could be an accomplished apprentice. If you want to build a new career, in 365 days you could already have finished one or more of the courses. Time is going to go by; there's no stopping it...so whether you use it to your advantage or not, 365 days will come and go. Where will you be 365 days from now? In the same place, or in the middle of building your dream?

7. If you don't have a dream, make one. Give some serious thought to what you want in your life. Yes, go ahead and make that crazy list. After you've listed all 99 ideas, pick out the top five. Which ones will make you happy? We live in a fascinating time, and most things are possible that weren't possible just 10 years ago. What's cool is that the things that look impossible today could very well be possible 10 years from now. So think about how you want to spend your life; at the other end of your path we all know we'll look back and see the way we've come. My advice is you find the milestones that bring you joy and the knowledge that you've lived a life of value. When I say that, I mean a life that's had value not only to yourself, but to others, too.

8. Make a plan, set goals, and every day take one step forward. If you don't know where you're going, you're going to spend a lot of time getting there. You also need to be ready for challenges and adjustments. You've heard that airplane pilots flying from

Seattle to Hawaii have to adjust their flight instruments many times during the trip. They know where they're going, but they have to allow for the variety of influences on the aircraft...wind, storms...a plan is a good roadmap because it shows you how to get to your destination. Then you have to be flexible enough to keep adjusting your path as you work forward toward your goals.

9. In all your actions, be positive. When you exhibit sincere interest and a cheerful outlook on life, people are more responsive to you, more willing to be open and friendly. You can always accomplish more with a good attitude than you can with a sour one. Show people you're really interested in them. "Nobody cares how much you know until they know how much you care"; that's one of my favorite quotes from Teddy Roosevelt. Another good thing you can do is smile more. Many of us tend to get lost in our thoughts and lose awareness of where we are and what we're doing. Stay present, feel the joy inside yourself and share it by smiling. You'll be amazed at the changes in people around you.

10. Remember to be a good role model. Do the right thing, say the right thing, be the best leader you can be. All of us have troubles, all of us have a struggle on our hands, but we also have the ability to rise above our never-ending anxieties. This is what it's all about, being as big as we know we can be, being as caring as we know we can be, being our own best fan by nurturing the love within and sharing it with everybody we meet.

11. Oh, yeah, Number 11: Never go past a lemonade stand without buying some.

12. We have to have 12, right? Here it is: Remember to smile! Smiles are contagious and a sincere smile can change your day. Try it!

This wasn't so wacky after all, was it?

My TV Show, "The Big Sports Lo-Down"

I was getting a deep tissue massage from my good friend Dale Newman at the Massage Clinic when my phone rang. It was my buddy, Tony DeLisio, a really great artist, graphics designer and one heck of a guitarist. I was introduced to two people on the phone, Daniel and Alan, who were starting their own Internet TV station and wanted me to get involved. We talked for a few minutes, and I agreed to meet them at their studio in Maple Valley the next day.

The next morning I drove out to Maple Valley, and after we met and exchanged some pleasantries, they showed me their professional recording and television studio. It turned out that Daniel's son, Jacob, was 12 years old and wanted to do his own sports show. Daniel wanted me to help his son with this project and be Jacob's co-host, and Daniel also wanted me to host my own sports show. I'd wanted to do my own radio and TV show for a long time, but I never had the chance. This looked like my opportunity!

Things got off to a bumpy start. Our opening date was scheduled for March, but we didn't launch until about mid-June. We were broadcasting on Blog Talk Radio and my show was called the Seattle Sports Lo-Down. The show ran for a few weeks and it was a lot of fun to be myself and talk about whatever sports I wanted to. I could pick the topics, the guests, and I loved the free flow of discussion, ideas and humor.

My other focus was on Jacob's show because I had agreed to help him and I wanted Jacob to have a good show. I contacted a few baseball players I knew and asked if they'd be willing to be interviewed by Jacob. Of course, this had "cute" written all over it, and they were very willing. I took Jacob to Safeco Field, and he got to record a few interviews. We also did an interview with Jeremy Bryant, the chef for the Mariners and the owner of Rain City Catering. We sat in the dugout and made some recordings there, too. Before we could put Jacob's show on the air, there was a parting of the ways. Daniel and Alan didn't see eye-to-eye on things, and eventually the relationship ended and, unfortunately, Jacob's show never aired. Then we were broadcasting just my show. Most of the recording was done at the studio, but we also had mobile cameras for interviews at remote locations.

We had a great technician; Xan Dewar was an amazing guy; he ran the boards, edited, and was my do-everything-guy. There was also Bill Cox who seemed to do everything Xan didn't do. We had a couple of other cameramen, Ross and Hyun, who went around with us. During the 14 months we were broadcasting, I went to several golf tournaments and interviewed a bunch of celebrity golfers, welcomed a number of interesting guests to the show, and had a lot of fun making some really cool shows. You can view these shows on YouTube by searching Big Sports Lo Down.

Everything came to a screeching halt one day. That was when I was doing a big story at Seafair taping interviews with the hydroplane drivers, the owners, and the spectators. I got really sick because I was on an antibiotic, and was supposed to stay out of the sun. While we were waiting for our press credentials, I was standing in the direct sunlight and it was over 90 degrees. We waited for almost two hours and the sun really hit me hard. I was also in direct sunlight rather frequently during the next two days.

I developed an abscess in the back of my leg that got infected, and the next thing I knew, a few days later, during the races, a gentleman told me I had blood running down my leg. I realized I'd better take care of myself, and it was worse than I thought. I was in the hospital for 27 days straight, with a short release and then another two weeks! I couldn't do the show, of course, but Alan said I shouldn't worry, and he assured me that they'd restart the show when I got better.

After taking about three months to heal up, we started the show again and I had several outstanding studio guests. I was able to bring former Seahawks quarterback Dave Krieg on the show, and Roy Lewis, Shawn Kemp, Gary Payton, and a whole lot of extraordinary athletes calling in or visiting the studio. This was the really cool time for my show because now we were broadcasting from the virtual set that Tony DeLisio had designed. Tony made this incredible virtual set that had the Seattle skyline at night with these amazing side boards. The set was surreal! I felt like I was on the major networks! It was just spectacular... This had been a dream of mine, to be involved in sports media, and now this dream had materialized! It was the most exciting feeling!

One of my broadcasting rules was to never speak badly about our team or any team, and to keep the comments positive and inspiring. This wasn't easy to do! People have very strong opinions about teams and individual players, and I got to experience what it was like to be under fire!

The Russell Wilson story was a huge topic. I had so many people calling in and saying that Wilson was a terrible choice as our quarterback. It was Russell Wilson this, and Russell Wilson that! I kept saying, "Wait a minute! You just watch! This guy's going to be something special for the Seahawks, and for years to come!" Even some of my best friends were telling me, "Hey! We signed Matt Flynn! We wouldn't have brought Flynn in for nothing, you know, just to sit around. Flynn should be the starting quarterback!" I kept telling them, "Stop! You just watch. Russell Wilson is going to be our starter, and he's going to be great!" Sure enough, Russell Wilson was our starter, and we've done great ever since.

Russell Wilson's college career showed his potential for the NFL. He was an incredible football player. Starting at North Carolina

State, he played there for two years and then transferred to Wisconsin. He took the Badgers to the Rose Bowl and played an incredible game. Watching his career, you could see the kind of a person he was. He's a gentleman, he's a winner. Guys like that are the kind of people you want around you, and on your team. In looking at all the positive qualities this kid had, it felt good supporting and believing in him. It was about the fifth or sixth week of the season when Russell had some struggles. Immediately everybody is calling for his head; "Bench him! Bench him!" ...but Coach stuck with him and eventually he ended up taking them to the "Big Show".

In spite of all the conflicting opinions that are part of the sports world, my show focused on the positive. I love doing things in a positive manner, and I'd rather see smiling people than angry people! When I was a bartender, people would always laugh and say I should avoid talking about sports, politics, and religion. That was good advice, too, because whenever sports, politics, or religion were brought up in the bar, somebody ended up yelling or swinging at somebody else!

You can imagine what it's like when you're doing a sports show! I learned to watch what I was saying, and keep the conversation entertaining while still giving my opinion. I did a pretty good job, too, because we had more fun than uproars. Many topics were discussed on my show, and there were a lot of good opinions on both sides of the issues; it was fun to be in the center of all that controversy! The show lasted until April 2013 when Alan's wife was offered a professional opportunity in India, so the studio was shut down and they moved away.

At that point, our numbers were really good. We had about 1,200 downloads a week and every time we asked for callers, we'd have people on the line, so we knew we were doing something right. I loved this incredible new role. I feel I did a pretty good job and I'd love to do it again!

Me and Russell Wilson Do a Commercial

I was sitting around one evening when my buddy Kenny called and said some people from Wongdoody, the local Seattle ad agency, were looking for fans to be in an Alaska Airlines commercial with Russell Wilson.

The next day I called up the company and spoke to a lady about the commercial and what they had in mind. She said I was going to be sitting in an airline seat next to Russell Wilson, asking him rapid-fire questions. Well, this sounded like fun!

A few weeks went by and I hadn't heard anything, so I thought, "Oh, well, I guess that faded out," but the next day there was a phone call. "Can you be here tomorrow at 10:00 a.m.?" Absolutely! I was totally honored that I'd be in a commercial with Russell Wilson! I'd met him a year before, but this time I'd be working with him on a set. I was excited!

When I got to the location, I found out I'd be doing a commercial not only with Russell Wilson, but also with Mama Blue, the original Seahawks Super Fan. When I was a kid, I idolized her. She's an incredible woman and she's been our team's #1 cheerleader since the very beginning. Of course, Russell had seen Mama Blue and me in the stadium many times before; I'm always in the end zone about 40 feet away when he's warming up, and Mama Blue is always on the corner where the team walks on and off the field. This was getting better and better! A star quarterback and two Super Fans!

We were told the commercial was based on a contest that had been held for fans who lived outside Washington. The commercial was to show Russell flying on Alaska Airlines to "rescue" the winners, and bring them back to Seattle for the Seahawks playoff games. When we filmed the first pair of winners, we had to go on location to the airport and cheer them as they walked through the gates. Of course, Russell wasn't there with us, but it was loads of fun anyway, seeing the expressions on the winners' faces, so excited about going to the playoff games and experiencing the 12th Man atmosphere. Being part of this commercial was very special; it's not something you get to do every day!

This commercial was shot in one day, with the main part being filmed at the Microsoft studios and just the one crowd-shoot at the airport. When it was our turn, Mama Blue and I sat on either side of Russell in a three-seat airplane row. There was no script, and we were told that all we had to do was just ask Russell rapid-fire questions, whatever came to our minds...within reason.

Mama Blue started off with, "Are we going to win the Super Bowl?" and I followed with, "What was your favorite breakfast cereal as a kid?" and she said, "Can I give you a kiss on the cheek?" and I said, "Can I give you a kiss on the cheek?" and we just played with it and had some fun. At one point I asked him, "What would you think if you had a blocker my size?" and Russell said, "I would love that!"

We had a whole lot of fun playing around, but then afterwards, I felt bad because all the Alaska Airlines employees bombarded Russell, asking him for autographs and photographs, and I could see in his face that he hadn't signed up for that; he'd come to only do a commercial. It turned into a bummer for him and I felt sad for his having to put up with this, but he was a good sport about it all, being his usual kind and diligent self. As he was signing autographs, I caught his eye and I said, "If you're done, just let me know," and Russell nodded, so I said, "Okay, guys, let's let him out of here," and I made a path for him, just like a big blocker, and helped him get out to his car. Russell signed a football for me, got in his car and away he went.

The funny thing is that the part of the commercial with Mama

Blue and I never aired on TV. For some reason it got pulled out of the lineup and no one ever got to see it. My guess is that someday it will be discovered in a storeroom somewhere, and then we're all going to have a big laugh!

Our Championship Season!

Our championship year began with our first game against the Panthers, and it was a road game. Everybody gets so worried about the 'Hawks when they have to go on the road because it seems we've always had that monkey on our back. "We can't win any games on the road..."

In this first game we were going up against Cam Newton, and the Panthers were supposed to be a really good team under his direction, but we pulled out a 12-7 win by the skin of our teeth, and this was important because it was the first win of the season on the road. Everybody was really excited about that.

It was on to Week 2 and we were playing against the San Francisco 49ers. We always want to beat the 49ers! This was a home game so we knew we were going to play them well, and we wound up winning in a decisive manner, smashing them 29-3. The year was starting to progress just right. Now we were 2-0.

Everyone was looking at each other and thinking, "Okay, well, how far can this go?" We beat the Jaguars in Week 3, and the Texans in Week 4. Now we were 4-0, and two of these games were on the road. Everyone was really interested by this time, wondering if we could go 5-0 for the first time in team history. That's when we went to Indianapolis where Andrew Luck had a great game and played hard against us, and we lost on the road to the Colts by six.

Oh, well. We were still a very strong team, and we weren't going to let one game get in our way! Week 6 was a home game against the Tennessee Titans and we barely beat them. Even though we won by only seven points in that game, now everyone could see the character of our team. "Wow, the Seahawks are a tough team to beat..."

And so the season went, beating the Cardinals, the Rams, the Buccaneers, Falcons, and the Vikings. We'd won six games in a row, and by Week 12 we were 10-1. Not bad. Not bad at all. In fact, pretty darn good!

We got to enjoy a bye week and then in Week 13 we faced the New Orleans Saints who were supposed to be able to play well against us. We manhandled them 34-7.

That took us to Week 14 and we were in San Francisco against the 49ers. Sometimes our team has a tough time playing there; as usual, there's a lot on the line. I don't usually go to the bar to watch a game, but I missed my old friends at Bleachers Pub where I used to work, so I went there to see that game. I enjoyed hanging out with my friends, and Shane, my buddy and old boss, and it was fun being with everybody...except we ended up losing that game by a hair, 17-19. That was really frustrating because I don't like losing to San Francisco, right? But it was what it was.

It was Week 15 and we took on the Giants, beating them by 23-0. Now we were 12-and-2 and we're looking at a really good season! We had a solid team, our defense was phenomenal and the offence was starting to get into their own rhythm. We ended up losing in Week 16 at home against the Cardinals and so, you know, a few people got depressed about it, but most people were really positive, saying, "It's just one game, just one game...we just have to beat the Rams." Ugh. The Rams!

In the last week of the regular season, the Rams came to town... and we beat them 27-9, ending our season with a convincing 13-3. Now we were going into the playoffs as the top dog in the NFC, and we had the home-field advantage throughout the playoffs. Everybody was amped up because we're at home for all the big games. This was huge!

The playoffs are always a different kind of animal, because some days you can play really well and some days you can play really bad. Even so, we had an excellent team. In the first playoff game, we beat the New Orleans Saints 23-15. Then we faced the San Francisco 49ers for the third time and beat them 23-17 in one of the most traumatic games you could ever imagine! It was amazing being at the stadium and watching what unfolded before our eyes! In the closing minutes of the game, the 49ers are driving down the field and they were one play from winning; Colin Kaepernick threw the ball up and Crabtree was right there...but up jumps Richard Sherman and tips the ball away! Everybody was screaming! It was amazing to know that we were going to the Super Bowl, to the Big Game!

This was our second shot at it, and I don't know if this team was any better than the team in 2005. I'd say this team was better-rounded, but you just can't compare them. Hey! I don't want to start a controversy! Both teams got there, and that's what counts. It was a great season, and all of us got to experience it together as fans.

It was amazing to be a part of something so magical and have that feeling, the feeling of winning, of being the best. That's the gift your team can give you, and that's why I'm such a strong fan. There are many great feelings to have in this life, and each one has its own special qualities and its own richness. To live a full life, it's important to sample every one of them, and when you take this success and happiness and achievement inside, it can help build all the other aspects of your life and your connections with people. This is how a fan can use that enthusiasm and excitement for the good of our communities and nation. Truthfully, you don't need to win a playoff game to have this personal energy and power. This passion is available to us all the time, when we tune into it. I think sports teach us all a good lesson about how to be committed, how to be loyal, and how to show love. At least, that's how I feel it's working in my life.

I spent the next two weeks trying to figure out how to get to New

Jersey to see The Game. During the playoffs, my buddy Kenny and I had made promises to throw a big Super Bowl party at The Hawks Nest Bar & Grill on First Avenue, and we'd been talking up a storm, inviting lots of people to a party we might ditch! As we were thinking about how to get to New Jersey, I was wondering how we're going to let all these people down if we really do make a cross country run. It turned out I didn't have to worry about it because Kenny's got a wife and a daughter, Jessica and Kaylin, and it wasn't something he could do anyway. He couldn't just say, "See you later, Honey, I'm going!"

When we reached that conclusion, we started going hard on planning this party, and we put it out there big-time, and everybody was very responsive about our staying in town and throwing this party. On the Big Day, we had about 500 people in a 200-person bar, and the place went absolutely berserk during the game. People started lining up at 7:00 a.m. By 10:30 there were probably 200 people in line to get in! I was happy to see the excitement in the hundreds of fans who wanted to come in and enjoy the game with each other. It was an amazing feeling.

Once the doors opened, the party started! I mean, the party really started outside on the streets because everybody who was waiting to get in was in a festive mood. The beer flowed like water, there was food everywhere, and everybody was yelling and shouting, all of us just waiting for the game to begin. While we waited, we had contests and prizes. We gave out tons and tons of Skittles and lots of people won tons of stuff like autographs, prizes from beer distributors, gifts from the Skittles people, beer signs, a beer cooler, signed photographs, hats, shirts, T-shirts from Jacknut Apparel, and the Seahawks had donated wristbands and flags and necklace things and there was just oceans of stuff to give away.

I was on the microphone that day, firing up the crowd and singing, and just go, go, going, and we had some musicians come in. Kevin Cartier, a local hip hop artist, came in and performed.

We had the Jet Cities Chorus come in and they sang the National Anthem... it was just out of control. We had a really good party and we pulled it off, and it was a lot of fun for everybody; even the local police walking around outside were having a good time!

The Hawks Nest has plenty of TVs in there. We were done with all the pregame shows, and all the ceremonial activities, and the coin toss, and then it was time for the kickoff! The game was starting! From that very first Peyton Manning snap when the ball went flying by him into the end zone and all of a sudden it's a safety and we were up 2 to 0. Then in no time at all we were up 9 to 0, then we were up, oh, I don't even remember how far up we were before the Broncos finally scored, and it was an astonishing and sensational wonder to witness! At half time we were 22 to 0. Absolute domination! Then the kickoff right after the first half, watching Percy Harvin find his way from where he caught that ball all the way down to the Bronco's end zone, well, the crowd inside the bar just went absolutely bonkers! All of us were screaming and laughing and going nuts! Everybody knew this was our day! This is the Seahawks' game! There's no way anybody's going to come back from that big a deficit and beat us in the Super Bowl! We just kept putting the boots down.

At the end of the third quarter the Broncos scored a touchdown and a 2-point conversion, and that was all they got. The score was 36-8. We just kept going and going! The whole time the crowd in the pub, and I mean everybody, was high-fiving, hugging, friends or complete strangers, and then when the game was over the party rolled out into the streets. There was an unending line of cars down First Avenue and everyone wanted to high-five you! Everybody wanted to hug you! The feeling of jubilation for this city, finally winning the Big Game, the one thing football fans strive for in every team's city, was here, finally, for Seattle, for our team, and we were the Champions of the World! There is no better feeling than that.

My buddies, Kenny and Jessica, and a couple of other friends stayed downtown as long as we could. We'd arrived about 7:30 in the morning and left about 11:00 at night. We had a celebratory dinner and enjoyed the rest of the night together, savoring everything about that wild, unbelievable, and hugely satisfying moment. That was a long day, and one of the very best!

The Super Fan in You!

I have an important message to share. You've probably caught glimpses of it throughout this book but I want to make it as clear as a football going through the center of the uprights.

Because sports are so important to so many millions of people around the globe, celebrity athletes have an amazing opportunity to influence people, especially children, in a way most of us can't.

Regional athletes, such as the quarterbacks of successful college football teams, have cameras and microphones thrust under their noses with reporters asking questions about the team, the game, the team's prospects, and all the usual questions we're used to hearing on sports shows or the evening news.

National sports celebrities on professional football, basketball, baseball, soccer, and hockey teams also receive wide public interest on what they have to say about the season and the team's expectations for the rest of the year.

This is all well and good, but I believe these athletes are missing a golden opportunity to influence our children and inspire all of us to improve our lives.

When an athlete is on the regional, national or international stage, I think the athlete should say a few words about the importance of good character. We are strongly influenced by the messages we receive from celebrity-level people, and when these athletes say something positive, such as how their success is a result of self-discipline, or a few words about their respect for their coach's leadership, or their dedication to practicing relentlessly, or affirming their responsibility for being a good role model on and off the field, or a short message about showing kindness and compassion for those less fortunate, we would see a thrilling transformation in our country. Regular messages like these from media celebrities will go a long way toward improving the way we treat each other, and will enhance the quality of all our lives.

The media has a huge impact on us, and I believe the media can be enlisted to help us spread the positive messages we need to hear so people are encouraged to make good choices and show good character. It wouldn't take much. If every athlete could say just one positive message about their sacrifice, or dedication, or gratefulness, and this happened every time an athlete spoke into a microphone, I believe we would see a happier and more productive society.

I'd like to see our nation's high schools and universities offer classes on media interaction so our young people are taught how to speak to an interested public while also sending a positive message that inspires our community or nation to influence ourselves and each other with the power of good character.

Of course, this means our young people need to be taught about good character, and this is a subject few of us have studied. This book is not the place for me to launch into an essay about good character; perhaps that will be my second book...but I believe that good character is essential to the well-being of our nation, our communities, our families, and ourselves.

When I was growing up, Dad taught me about good character. I learned to have a high regard for honesty, respect for my elders and family and friends, to always play fair, to be responsible for my actions, and to care about other people's feelings and property. School taught me about citizenship, and my coaches taught me about leadership and self-discipline.

I learned to show appreciation for people who did nice things for me, and how important it is to help others. I also try to do at least one nice thing for somebody every day, and usually I do a dozen. I've also learned to be grateful for what I have and kind to everyone I meet.

It's really all about being a good person, and making good choices. Most of us are good and decent people, and most of us want to do the right thing. Of course, if drugs or alcohol get in the way, everything changes; those are negatives that corrupt our ability to think clearly and make good decisions. I know this was true in my case.

When I was a kid living at home, I was under Dad's influence, and I followed his rules and behaved the way I was taught. When I got out on my own, like most young adults, I had a lot of exploring to do, and some of those paths led me astray. I was influenced by drugs and alcohol, and I did some pretty stupid things. Even though my drug of choice was only marijuana, it was still a negative influence in combination with my drinking and partying attitudes.

As early as high school I had hostility issues; drugs and drinking were a factor. I took my aggression out on the football field, and as you know, for other reasons, I was dropped from the football team the week of our quarter finals game in my senior year, and because of my attendance, I didn't graduate with my class. After high school I began working in the clubs as a bouncer, and my drinking continued. For most people, and it's true for me, in this culture our young adults spend their 20s trying to figure out what they want to do with their lives. Some people know right away, and they have the drive to reach their goals. For others, it takes some false starts to finally wind up on the right path.

Being a bouncer allowed me express my hostility and violent temper as a protector of the people I cared about and the people I was hired to protect. I wasn't going to let my friends or coworkers get hurt, and if I saw someone doing something bad to them, I took over and put a stop to it. When I was about 25 or 26 I decided I didn't like drinking anymore because it made me mean. I turned off the switch and quit drinking, and I did it cold turkey. Once I stopped drinking, I became a nicer person and I took more time to think about things. Instead of throwing the first punch, I'd analyze a situation and talk my way out of fights, not into them. At that point in my life, I wanted to be the good guy instead of the bad guy. I think it's easier to be the good guy; I'd rather make a smile than a frown, and that's what I'm about today. I was able to step outside myself and take a good look, and I wasn't happy with what I saw or felt. That's when I made the decision to switch gears.

When I did that, I noticed that my attitude changed, my friends changed, my outlook on life improved, and I began to realize I could do more than I'd been doing, that I had a lot of passion and strength in me, and I wanted to use my energy in positive ways that helped people. That's when I became an afterschool coach and learned to offer the kindness and compassion that has guided my life ever since. I'm always going to strive to be a better person because I want to help as many people as I can, so they can achieve their own personal success and then use their strengths and abilities to help even more people.

This is why I believe good character is so important. We have multiple opportunities every day to make good choices. We can choose to live in darkness, or we can choose to bring in the Light. I'm going to do my best to make choices that help me be a champion every day.

Help Me Start the Seattle Hall of Fame

I believe Seattle needs its own Hall of Fame, a museum dedicated to all the professional and collegiate sports teams we have in our state. If I could do things my way, I'd like to have a sports restaurant like John Howie's Sport Restaurant over on 4th Avenue...but I also feel Seattle would benefit from a place where people can go and reflect...reflect on the value of sports, athleticism, statistics, world-class records, and on the triumph of the human body and the human spirit. This would be a place to inspire our young athletes, and a shrine, almost, to the glory of Northwest sports. I'm surprised we don't already have one, and I think it's about time we did!

When you think about it, we have a lot of sports history here. We had the Metropolitans who won the Stanley Cup in 1917, and the Pilots who became the Milwaukee Brewers. We had the Thunderbirds, the Storm, the Sonics...and now we have a wide range of teams with the Redhawks, Silvertips, Rollergirls, Force, Grizzlies, Majestics, Mist and Mountaineers...the list goes on. We've got athletes in swimming, tennis, archery, cycling, martial arts...there is a lot of sports activity in our area and almost no place to gather and display this rich sports heritage. Doesn't this make you wish you could see all the amazing artifacts and history in one place? I do!

I've got a lot of memorabilia I'm willing to put in glass cases for everyone to enjoy. I've got bases from actual baseball games, game-used footballs, game-worn jerseys, and a lot of signed jerseys. I've got thousands and thousands of autographed items: baseballs, photographs, sports cards, all of them accumulated over the years from being a sports fan. I've got game-worn shoes from LeBron James and Kobe Bryant. I also have Brandon Roy's first shoes as an NBA player in his first game with the Portland Trail Blazers against the Sonics. Jason Terry's game shoes, Shawn Marion's, Shaquille O'Neal's, and those are some pretty big shoes! I've got some pretty small ones, too... and tons and tons of stuff. I've got over 400 pairs of shoes, and at least 500 signed baseballs. Plus, I have signed footballs, basketballs, soccer balls... I've even got a hockey stick signed by Ken Caminiti, the National League's Most Valuable Player. He played hockey in college so I got a hockey stick and I asked him to sign it because I thought that would be kind of cool.

I've got a really funny item signed by Ryan Leaf, the former quarterback. It was when he got in trouble for being mean to the media; it's a really sour picture of him on the front page of the sports section. Everybody was trying to get him to sign it and he wouldn't sign it for anybody. I folded the newspaper in half and put it in front of him and he signed it without knowing what it was. It's pretty cool because the photo shows him being a knucklehead...and he signed his name to it!

I have a number of treasured items. Some of them are priceless to me. Nate McMillan gave me his Finals shoes from the playoffs in 1996. I've also got one of Michael Jordan's shoes from a Finals game in 1996. I've got the very last pair of shoes that Matt Hasselbeck ever wore as a Seattle Seahawk. I've got Super Bowl jerseys from Marcus Trufant and Matt Hasselbeck. I've got a lot of stuff! I've also got the old end zone pads from the goal posts at the Kingdome.

I've never been to a sports Hall of Fame...that's on my bucket list, but when I have the funding, I'd like a football-shaped building and a soccer ball-shaped building and a basketball-shaped building...well, I don't know if you could really build a baseball bat-and-ball building because that would be kind of weird, but there are a lot of different design ideas to think about. I would love it if the museum was like the inside of Cabella's with the little streams flowing and fish swimming along, and then all of a sudden you walk up to a display case with curious memorabilia...

I was a collector when I was a child, too, and saved all my sports cards; I had Mickey Mantle cards, Joe DiMaggio cards, Yogi Berra cards, and I had all these different collections. I had game shoes from players way back in the '70s and autographs...I had a ton of stuff that my uncle and cousins had given me. I moved out of my dad's house when I was 18 and left all of it behind. My stepmother and I didn't get along and I procrastinated on moving all the boxes out. I waited too long and one day she decided I didn't need that stuff anymore and she threw it all out...which today would be worth tens of thousands of dollars. But that's what happens as we get older; we lose things along the way. Wouldn't it be great if there was a Seattle Hall of Fame where every kid's collectibles could be displayed for everyone to enjoy?

Support My Foundation, Dude

I was a coach for about a dozen years, and I probably spent thousands and thousands of dollars to help pay sports participation fees for kids who needed help. At Interbay, we could only offer so many scholarships, and this was true on Queen Anne Hill, too. A lot of our neighbors could use a helping hand, and we don't want their kids to suffer or miss out on an opportunity that could make a big difference in their lives. I mean, would you rather have a gang of kids who are excited about being on a team, and exercising, and having good attitudes...or would you rather just have a gang?

While I was coaching in the after-school programs, I met these incredibly talented kids. Many of them came from homes and family lives in disarray. I know it must seem hard to believe that, especially if your home and family life is solid. It was hard for me to believe it, yet I saw it constantly. Either their parents didn't give a darn, or the parents were in jail, or their parents had passed away. There's more people struggling than you realize, and it's especially tough on the kids. A lot of these kids are left to fend for themselves. Once they start eating poorly, can't perform properly in school, start sampling alcohol and drugs, have no creative outlet for their energy except getting in trouble...well, you can see where that will lead.

I had this feeling in my heart that I wanted to do something for them, let them see there was more to life than the box they were trapped in, and I stepped up to keep these kids involved in sports and involved with the after-school activities. I saw them come to these programs, and they were happy, excited, eager to be a part of a team and work together. For some of these kids, I'm sure it was the best part of their day. Then, as the sky got dark, I'd watch them exit the playing fields and wander down the streets, getting in trouble and doing this and that. It started my wheels turning on how I could better their situation and make some sort of contribution that would add hope to their lives.

Many of these boys and girls don't have a big brother or a big sister to help them, let alone a father figure. It's so important that these kids know somebody in the big wide world cares about them and can help them grow in a positive and healthy manner. I know we can't fix all the world's ills, but I believe we can fix some, and that's what I want my foundation to do. I hope you'll see the value of helping our youth and you'll contribute your kindness, your time, and your money.

My goal this year is to start the SHY Foundation, the Sandretzky Helping You Foundation.

The mission of the foundation is to help kids by paying their sports activity fees, and equipment, if they need it.

Something I learned by being Santa's Biggest Helper is the joy of doing something good for somebody. Over the last 10 years I've been helping raise money for decorations and presents and dinner for these families, and it's been a blessing and an amazing feeling to know that my small and simple activities have meant so much to people who have so little.

I know I can do more, and since you're reading this, I'm inviting you to join me. I'm planning to start the SHY Foundation in January 2015. I'll be sending messages out through Twitter, letting you know that the foundation has been established and that we're collecting tax-deductible funds to help the children. If you'd like to volunteer a few hours per week or per month to help the foundation, please contact me. I can think of no better way to help our community than by supporting our children and providing a better chance for a good life.

Get Down with Big Lo

1. You have two cars that are covered with decals. What can you tell us about them?

I've got two cars; one is a '94 Grand Cherokee Limited, and the other is a 2000 Grand Cherokee Limited. When I met Christian from Jacknut Apparel in 2009, he told me his father, Rick, owns Coastline Signs out in Aberdeen. They put their heads together and said, "Let's wrap Big Lo's vehicle, and get some sports stuff on it," so they decorated the Jeep. A couple of years down the road, we wrapped the second Jeep. We worked out the designs together, and the Jeeps have logos and designs for the Seahawks, Sounders, Mariners, the Storm, the Seattle Mist, the Seattle Timberwolves, and the Washington Stealth.

The design that rocks me the most is the Sonics headstone on the rear quarter panel; it lists the years the Sonics were here, and the headstone says Rest in Peace. That's my favorite tribute on the car.

There is also a Coastline Signs decal, a Jacknut Apparel decal, and an Ila's Foods decal. Ila's Foods is in Hoodsport and they make delicious jams, jellies, and dressings; they're great. The cars still have room for more logos, so if you want to be a sponsor, hit me up!

2. What's your favorite type of music?

As far as music goes, I love all kinds. There isn't any music I won't listen to, except hard-core rap. The lyrics are usually harsh, and I feel women deserve more respect than that.

On the lighter side, there are times when I love listening to Dad play the accordion; I've been doing that since I was a kid. The accordion is an amazing instrument.

Modern rock 'n roll and heavy metal is what I like the most, from bands like Iron Maiden, *Queensryche, and Dio.*

Locally, I like Mechanism, which is Tony DeLisio's band. Tony's music has been a big part of my life because I've known him for so long, and I used to help him carry his equipment back in the day. I also did security for him, and I've seen his progress from Gypsy Rose, his first band, all the way up to his current band, Mechanism. In my opinion, Tony is the best lead guitarist I've ever heard; he's a hell of a guitar player and I have a lot of respect for Tony and his music.

3. What kind of books do you like to read?

I like books that have anything to do with sports. One biography I read that was really outstanding was Tony Gwynn's book, "San Diego Baseball". I saw Tony in a local bookstore doing signings, so I got a signed copy. His book was fascinating, all about his life story and his upbringing. One of the saddest days of my life was when he passed away on June 16, 2014.

4. What are some of your all-time favorite movies?

Movies require being in a special mood, so the movies I enjoy depend on the mood I'm in. At times I can be romantic, and at other times I can be a fanatic, but generally I like anything with Samuel L. Jackson, and almost anything with Adam Sandler.

Of course, I like movies about sports and athletes! "Gridiron Gang" with The Rock is one of my favorites, and so is "He Got Game" with Ray Allen. I also like "Rudy" with Sean Astin in the starring role. I met Sean once when we were doing a sports show together at King 5.

5. What type of art is your favorite?

I'm the best stick figure artist you'll ever meet! I'm also pretty good with pinch pots. The pinch pot I made in the third grade was the ugliest in the class...

I love visual art and I'm fascinated by the talents that some people have. I love to see what people have created, and I respect all types of art.

My sister Marlee and my dad were the two that were blessed with artistic talent. Marlee was good at drama and drawing. Bonnie was in the choir.

My performance art was singing, and I played a lot of different instruments: bass, trumpet, saxophone, guitar, and some piano. I never could pick up the accordion; I just couldn't do it; I don't know how my dad does it. It's got a lot of buttons and keys!

I think the best artwork of all is our Earth, and what God created. Dad and I have taken off at 7 o'clock in the morning, sometimes not returning until 1:00 a.m. because we were driving up into the mountains and were captivated by the beauty. Mount St. Helens, Mt. Adams, Mt. Baker, Mt. Ranier... Dad and I have been all over the place looking at the beauty that God created. Dad instilled this love of nature in me; God created a beautiful planet, absolutely gorgeous.

6. Do you have any particular type of talent?

I've mastered being a sports fan!

Actually, I sang in my high school choir and we won the Best in the Northwest Choir Festival two years in a row, in 1983 and 1984. I have a pretty good tenor's voice! I've also won solo contests for my singing, and also national contests as a barbecue chef. One of these days I'm going to bottle my recipe; I'm looking for a business partner! I think we'll call it "Big Lo's Blitz" or "Big Lo's Moon Shot Sauce" or something sports-related like that.

7. What was the funniest moment in your life?

July 29, 1999.

It was my first time sitting behind home plate on the second level's front row at the Kingdome. That night I caught three out of four foul balls!

In the second inning, Russ Davis came up to the plate, fouled the ball up toward me and I made a dramatic one-handed catch over the rail about three feet down. I had to lean down to catch it, and the crowd went nuts! In the fifth inning, Manny Ramirez was up and I made a two-handed catch over the rail. Then, in the sixth inning, Russ Davis was up again and he hit a foul ball right into my chest. This one was also a two-handed catch. Each time I made the catch, the crowd went crazy.

On this catch, my third one, Brock Huard, who was then the Huskies quarterback, came down and said, "Man, I could use a tight end like you!" and he gave me a big thumbs up. Also, a lady came down and said she was from the TV show "This Week in Baseball", and if I caught one more foul ball, it would be a record and Ozzie Smith would have me on the show. The pressure was on!

In the eighth inning, the fourth ball came my way, and it was just above my head...I reached up nonchalantly...and felt it slip through my fingertips...so unfortunately, I missed that one. And the crowd booed me! OMG! "Come on, man, you know, I made these three beautiful catches and then all of a sudden I miss one. And you're going to boo me?"

Later I got a picture with Brock Huard and the balls, and that was a pretty cool thing. Oh yeah, I only had two of the balls left because I'd given the first one to a young fan who was sitting next to me. Catching the three foul balls was a momentous experience for me, and I also had the pleasure of making that kid's night!

8. Where were you when the Kingdome came down?

Oh, yeah! I was right there holding my own press conference! It was crazy. I had five cameras on me and about 13 microphones in front of me. It was the biggest media event I'd ever done. When the Kingdome went down, I cried like a baby. I was a big fan of the Dome. I grew up in that stadium, and I was wishing they would've slapped on a new coat of paint, and revamped the bathrooms, revamped all the suites, but they didn't listen to me. I loved that place. Heck, some of my childhood toys were in the ground underneath it.

By the way, my second biggest press conference was when they were building Seahawks Stadium in 2002. The management had picked out a bunch of different seats, and asked me to come down and try them out! My concern is always that you have to have enough room for big people, and at that time I wanted to make sure the seats fit my butt. The press was there to find out if I liked the new seats, and they fit like a glove!

9. What was your most favorite Christmas gift?

I received my most favorite Christmas gift when I was in my 20s. It was funnier than heck because I was with my family and everybody had already opened up their presents when Marlee said, "Oh, wait! I have one more thing for you." She disappeared for a moment and then brought out this big cardboard cutout about four feet tall, of the Energizer Bunny! I yelled, "Oh, my God! That is so awesome!" and I went absolutely nuts. Marlee got excited because it only cost her two bucks. Some of the best gifts are inexpensive.

10. If you could travel to any place on Earth, where would it be?

Before I die, I would love to go to Australia. Everything there seems so much different than here. The landscape, the people, the animals... Australia has always fascinated me.

11. What was your favorite toy as a kid?

My favorite toy was my Aurora AFX Track. I loved building the tracks and racing the cars. When we lived in our house in Kent, we had a spare bedroom and I took it over and made it into my track room. I had a huge layout and spent hours and hours in there. It was a lot of fun building the different layouts, getting new cars and trucks, tinkering with the track to make everything faster, and beating my buddies. I spent a lot of happy hours playing with my tracks and race cars.

12. Do you have a favorite flavor ice cream?

Absolutely! Baseball Nut® ice cream from Baskin-Robbins. They've had it since I was a kid. It's only seasonal, starting about the first part of baseball season and then it's gone by September. Oh, it's delicious!

I've always been a chocolate guy, too. The one-two tier is chocolate on the bottom and Baseball Nut® on the top. It's a home run in my mouth every time!

Epilogue

I hope you've enjoyed reading my book. I also hope some of the messages I shared with you have been helpful. My main goal for this book was to share some of the interesting experiences of my life, and also to inspire people to love and help each other more.

My story isn't finished. I've got a strong feeling I'll be around for another five or six decades at least, so if you like this book, you might enjoy my next couple of books, too. They won't all be about me because I want to write a book on sports for children, and another one that details the stories of all the amazing teams we have here in the Great Northwest.

I'm also going to have a whole lot more stories about my experiences as a Super Fan. You saw the photograph of me and Pete Carroll at the "We Are 12" exhibit honoring The 12th Man at the Experience Music Project museum in Seattle. My next Super Fan book will include this story and more.

I just finished recording a new song with my buddy Daryl Diamonds called "March On Lynch". I fed him the idea and he ran with it. We think it's pretty awesome! It's available now in iTunes at this link: https://itunes.apple.com/bw/album/march-on-lynch-feat.-big-lo/id932927155

You can also follow me on Twitter at @BigLo66 ... and on Instagram at /biglosuperfan

There are a few other things I have in mind, too. I'm
making plans to go to Glendale, Arizona, to see Super Bowl
XLIX. I also want to go to a NASCAR race, visit Australia,
and get back to broadcasting my own TV show. A really
important project is starting my new Sandretzky Helping
You Foundation so we can help the boys and girls in our
community know the joy of being part of a winning team,
and build their sense of purpose.

I wish you every joy and every happiness. I know the day
will come when we'll meet, and I would love to shake your
hand.

God bless!

Big Lo.

Made in the USA
Lexington, KY
29 April 2017